Voices

Bishop Auckland and West Auckland

Young Master Van den Berg, the son of a trapeze artiste, c. 1930.

Voices of
Bishop Auckland and West Auckland

John Land

First published in 1998 by Tempus Publishing

Reprinted in 2009 by
The History Press
The Mill, Brimscombe Port,
Stroud, Gloucestershire, GL5 2QG
www.thehistorypress.co.uk

ISBN 978 0 7524 1090 6

Typesetting and origination by
Tempus Publishing
Printed in Great Britain

Cover picture:
Workers in Farr's Yard, Bishop Auckland at the turn of the century. Managers and foremen wore
bowler hats as a symbol of their status.

The corner, on which the Eden Theatre stands, was, and remains, a popular meeting place in Bishop
Aukland.

CONTENTS

Scene from the filming of Near Home, at Wilsons forge.

INTRODUCTION

During twenty-five years of research into the history of Bishop Auckland, West Auckland and the surrounding districts the memories of many local people have been recorded. This is a collection of those memories, written in the words of the speaker. Recollections of the past are a precious part of our lives. We tend to believe that our memories are of personal interest only but, so often, these are the only record of the ordinary, everyday past. For these memories to be accessible is important if successive generations are to understand how the people of their home town thought, felt and lived.

Bishop Auckland, West Auckland and the surrounding villages played an important role in the Industrial Revolution. Relatively little has been written about this role, simply because the events are of a quite recent nature. In compiling this book I have been reminded of the fact that history is made every day and that that history is well worth recording. Though recent, in historical terms, the events recalled in the book are fascinating now and will become more so for the future.

I have been careful not to intrude into people's privacy. Many memories are very personal and have not been used except with the express permission of the contributor. The aim of this book is to interest and entertain and to record events in the every day lives of our ancestors, which would otherwise be lost. The people whose memories are recounted within this book have, without exception, been able to recall, in great detail, events from years gone by. It has been a privilege to share those moments. So often one memory triggers off another, which had lain dormant for many years, resulting in an absorbing discourse. It is hoped that these memories will bring pleasure to the reader and will stir the reader's own memory, as well as stimulating a greater awareness of our local history.

John Land, 1998.

When memory turns to bygone days there's much for sorrow much for praise

CHAPTER 1

Childhood and schooldays

School class, c. 1899. This is probably somewhere near Tindale. Billy Walton is the little boy on the front row, extreme left. His sister Lizzie is sitting next to him (second from the left) and another sister, Susan, can be seen in the third row from the front, fifth from the left.

Newfield School children, early this century.

St Annes School

I was born at 4 Adelaide Street, Bishop Auckland in 1910 and went to St Annes school down South Church Lane. The refrain of the school is

Be good sweet maid and let who
will be clever
Do noble things not dream them all
day long
And so makes lives endeavour last
for ever
One grand sweet song.

Miss Baron was headmistress of the infant school. It was a mixed infants, boys and girls. I moved to standard one when I was six and a half. I was one of the clever ones and I missed the top class of infants. The teacher was Miss Gibbon, standard two was Miss Storey; standard three was Miss Prescotte and in standard four it was Miss Neasham. Mrs

Sherwood came to standard five after Miss Dobson left. In standard six there was Miss Porritt and she lived in Princes Street. In standard seven it was Miss Harker and nobody liked her (she wasn't half handy with a ruler).

Miss Sherwood put this onion in a certain position, we had to paint it and she went round and looked at everybody's picture and said to me 'stand on the seat' and I thought, 'oh what's matter here?' and I stood on the seat. She said, 'Now everybody look at this girl she is the duaghter of a famous painters and decorators and this is what she paints for an onion.' I never felt so embarrassed in my life.

When you got into the jurors it was all girls. I left in 1924 and stayed at home until I was married. You see if I'd gone out to work when my brothers were on the dole the money was taken off you. My grandfather was in the painting and decorating business as Vart & Bellerby. My brothers were on the dole because in 1925 people couldn't afford to have their decorating done. My father died in the First World War and my mother had to bring up six children. My father was in the East Yorkshire Regiment.

My eldest brother got a job in Scarborough and we went there because his wife had died so my mother packed up her home. We were living at 7 Adelaide Street then, next to Vardy's fish and chip shop. Henry Vardy's – a fish and a pen'orth. My mother moved and I went with her. I stayed there until I was married and then we moved to Etherley. My husband's family were farmers at Etherley. We lived at No. 1 Bankwell, but don't get mixed up with Bankwell Drive. There was a well further down. I lived there for fifty years.

As a child I went to the United Methodists at the botton of Adelaide Street. I went to Sunday school, I think I was about five. We went on Sunday school trips and you went to the Band of Hope. There was something on at the chapel every night. When I got older we did concerts which I used to organise. I belonged to the Camp Fire Girls at the chapel. The Quakers had them as well. We used to sing songs and have talks.

When we lived in Adelaide Street I can remember the prisoners being walked, handcuffed, from the police station to the railway station on their way to the assizes at Durham along the street. with policemen walking with them.

Amy Hodgson (née Vart)

Eldon School

I was born at Close House 74 years ago, in a small house in Main Street next to the Cobblers Hut. From there we moved down the street and I went to Eldon School, which isn't there now. Another move to 19 Close House, which was great, plenty of back yard to play in and I then went to Black Boy School, which was the tops. I enjoyed my schooldays and attended Close House Methodist Chapel for a year. I enjoyed going to the chapel and the Quaker Sunday School. I never missed Sunday school which was full of very happy memories. My sister and I had our hats (all hand made) bought from the shop that Mrs Buckle had. We wore them at the Sunday school anniversaries, two Sundays a year which were wonderful.

D. Carrick

Barrington School

My brother Harold went to the Barrington School in the market place. He got a prize every year he was there for good manners. The headmaster was Mickey Bell.

Amy Hodgson

Firm But Fair

I went to the Barrington School. I started at Cockton Hill infants. My grandparents had the Sportsman Inn in the market place for many years. My father worked as a solicitor's clerk in Old Bank Chambers in the market place and my step-father was the manager of the Red Stamp Store, which is now Iceland Foods. The headmaster of the Barrington was Mr Keith Elland who was firm but fair. He once gave me six of the best for scrumping apples from the Bishops Palace gardens and said he should expel me for bringing disgrace to the school. The Bishop's butler had seen us and reported us to the school. Bob Hardesty, the famous footballer, taught me maths. He now has a street named after him in the town.

There was a handball pitch in the school playground and you can still see the line drawn across. We played pop alleys there. Then Mr Bert King came, he was an ex-army PT instructor and wore crossed swords on his vest. He got a wooden horse for vaulting and other equipment and trained us up. We were very fit at the time.

There was the Blue Boys Charity [Lord Crewe's Charity]. Poor children were given an article of clothing. I remember getting a pair of trousers. There were races on VE Day in the Bishops Palace with different schools competing. This was the first time I remember money given as prizes.

Trevor Davies

[*The Blue Coat Charity was founded by Bishop Lord Crewe in 1720. In addition he made a provision in his will 'to pay a further sum of thirty pounds yearly for the clothing of thirty poor boys'. The charity was administered by the minister and churchwardens of St Andrews, Auckland.*]

Jack Bake's Story

I asked my dad Jack Bake to give me information for my family history research and what he remembered of Bishop Auckland as a child. I asked him to make a tape and this is the story he told.

Gavin Blake

I was born on 16 December 1923. I was christened John Henry but I was always known as Jack. My mother was Winifred and my father was William but he was always known as Bop. He got thirty shillings on the dole and he had to have his share for cigarettes and his drink. Many times he would go for days to Newcastle, Hartlepool or any other place he could box and make some money, not to bring home, just for his drink and to be with his cronies. It didn't last long and my mother left him and went to grannys to live – Granny Morland.

I started school from my grannys and she made sure we got what we needed for clothes and food. Later on in life when I looked at the place where I was born, Dennisons Yard, I found I wouldn't let pigs live there.

Getting back to my grannys, it was a two bedroom house at 11 Thompson Street. My grandfather, he still worked down the pit. After going to two wars he finished up down the pit. It was always warm and there was plenty of food.

In those days there was a lot of people dying from infectious diseases such as diphtheria, rickets, meningitis and TB, things that's more easily cured today. If a woman who was pregnant didn't get the proper food, more or less the baby was born with rickets, it was a common sight in those days. My brother Wilfred and my sister Winifred both died of meningitis at the age of five.

I can remember going to our Wilfred's funeral in a horse-drawn carriage, friends and relatives walked behind. It was a common sight in those days, there were not so many cars knocking about or wagons, mostly horse-drawn carriages or three wheeler bikes.

On a Staurday night, when the men had gone out for their drink, me granny and two or three of her cronies would meet at me grannys. They would send me to the Harpy Inn [Harp Inn in Thompson Street] that was two doors away for a couple of cans of beer. They were dressed up, at least they thought they were dressed up, with their long skirts and their clean pinny's, that was the dress for the night. I can always remember one woman, with a flat cap on, smoking a pipe.

In those days a married woman with a family, it was out of the question her going out to work. Work in the house it was that demanding. It took a day to do the washing with the old fashioned poss tub and wringer. Granny did all her own baking with a dish in the middle of the floor and a stone of flour at a time. Another half day to do the fire, black lead the ashpan and the bars and metal polish all the fire irons. God help you if you sat on the fender.

I can remember starting school from me granny's. I was sitting on the table and she was fitting a new pair of boots on me. A little grey coat, short trousers, grey jumper with a tie. I was the bees knees. When they took me to school that morning they had to bring me back because they were changing the schools. St Annes, which had been a girl's school, and the Barrington, which was a boy's school, were both changing over to mixed schools. So the following day I went back. In my classroom the first thing they gave me was a slateboard, a pencil shaped slate – it was to draw on. The other thing was plasticine on a board. Not much education in those days I can tell you. When it came to the eleven plus if you passed you went to Grammar School, if you could afford things like the uniform, the books and the sports gear. So the majority went on to the Barrington and stayed there from eleven to fourteen. When you left school at 14 you went to a job, if there was a job for you, if not you went to the Dole School until there was a job for you. You could have gone on there until you were 18 years old.

If you lived outside the town you were allowed to bring sandwiches to school or otherwise you went home for your dinner. There was no such thing in those days as school dinners. I was never keen on school and went home for my dinner. I used to be still on the way home when the others were coming back. One day when I went home for my dinner me Uncle Harry was sitting on the step. He said, 'You can't come in here, because you don't live here anymore.' Apparently me Mam and Dad had got back together again and had got one room above an ice cream shop in Princes Street. They called this ice cream shop Panzeri's. It was right opposite the theatre. We didn't live there very long, but while we did live there I used to go out selling papers. At night, after me father had gone out, we used to put the lights out, open the bedroom window and we used to watch all the shows coming out of the theatre, the circuses and all that.

Anyway we moved away from there. We moved to a place in Tenters Street with a big yard, they called it Wisemans Yard. There were seven houses in the yard and we shared one tap. There was about five earth toilets. We lived in No. 6. It had one bedroom and one room downstairs and the tap was in the middle of the yard. The rest of the families living in the yard were all young couples and they all had kids about my age and believe you me they were all rough. For the first few weeks I was in more fights than enough with 'em. I would beat one then another would join in, but I soon got used to them. I was as rough as them and they accepted me in their gang and that's when I started growing up, in other words I was more or less a street urchin.

Jack Bake

A Young Entrepreneur

In those days money was in very short supply, you couldn't get much off your parents because they hadn't any. You might get the odd halfpenny or the odd penny, you needed all the money you had just to live on. So I used to make money by running messages, or go to the store and buy a couple of boxes of wood and chop them up, bundle them up in sticks and sell them at a halfpenny a bundle, otherwise I had nothing. I used to go to the golf links on a Wednesday afternoon and carry the golf clubs for the businessmen. I got a shilling, I used to give me mother a

tanner [sixpence] of that and the rest I used to enjoy myself with – pictures and sweets.

I used to run a lot of messages for a woman called Mrs Durham, Mr Durham used to keep pigs. I used to collect all the peelings from the fish shops and take them down where he kept his pigs, he used to give me one and six for that lot. So I used to earn my money, that's before I started work.

Jack Bake

One Good Turn

I'll always remember one day I was playing up the recreation ground when this boy about my age was walking through the rec. He had a briefcase under his arm. Anyway this gang of lads started teasing him. They took his briefcase off him and tossed it in the grass and he ran off home. Shortly after that they went away and left the briefcase in the grass so I went and picked it up and had a look inside, it was full of music sheets, apparently he'd been for music lessons up Etherley Lane somewhere. His name and address was in it so I decided to take it to him. He lived in Victoria Street, so off I went, rung the bell and this maid came out. When I think of her now she looked like Sue Pollard out of *Upstairs Downstairs*. Anyway she thanked me and said, 'wait there a minute'. She came out and gave me tuppence, fair enough. This lady who was standing in the kitchen could see me through the hallway and I'd got as far as the gate when she told me to wait a minute and she said, 'I've got something here that might fit you.' Champion. She said, 'Come in'. So I went in and she gave me a glass of pop. She went upstairs and she came down with these two carrier bags full of clothes and shoes. Anyway I took them home and what didn't fit me, fit our Larry. Me mother was over the moon. I used to have to wear them for school and also on Sunday, not on a night time - then I had to put me rags on. I went back to that house two or three times. It did help out believe you me.

Jack Bake

Pop Music

In the early thirties there was little in the line of entertainment, just picture halls and the wireless. Very few people had a wireless and they were battery operated. If you wanted to know all the songs of the day you would hear them on the pictures or on the wireless or you would have to go into Woolworths and buy a song sheet for a penny and we would learn all the songs. The picture halls were the Kings Hall, the Hippodrome and the Majestic, which became the Odeon [now gone], the Odeon wasn't even opened until 1956. The first film was A Yank at Oxford. I've seen me go in the pictures at the Kings Hall at six o'clock, watch the picture right through and in the next house fall asleep and come home at half past ten. If we didn't do that we were playing in the streets. The Hippodrome and the Kings Hall, in those days, were bug infested. We used to come out of there covered in bug bites. We used to go home and the homes we were living

Young Jack Bake, in his early days in the army.

in, they were infested an' all. If you were talking to a neighbour you could see the bugs crawling up the walls.

Jack Bake

Treats

Twice a year the businessmen of Bishop Auckland used to treat all poor children, once at Christmas and once in summer. We would get a Christmas party and an outing in the summer to the seaside, usually Seaton Carew. We used to all line up, hundreds of us and get on the buses. When we were on the bus, with a tag fastened to our lapel, we used to get tuppence and when we got there we got a bottle of pop, from Jones's, and a pork pie. At teatime they used to take us to this big hall, give us a bag of cake and a cup of tea - that was the summer outing.

At Christmas time they gave us a free show at the Hippodrome, then they used to march us down to the Town Hall, all of us with our pots. There were more pots smashed on the way down than enough. They used to give us cakes, pies and things like that. When we came out we got a bag of fruit and that was your treat for the year.

Jack Bake

A Clip Across The Ear

A year or so before a fellow called Hitler was shouting his mouth off in Germany, the people in the north east were that desperate, especially in the Jarrow area, that they decided to march on London. It started at Jarrow and picked up more men on the way down. I remember them coming through Bishop Auckland. They stayed in an old church in Russell Street. I remember them marching up Tenters Street, and believe you me it was a sorry sight. They got to London about a week after but for what good it did them they might as well have kept on marching.

Later on the Prince of Wales, Prince Edward - the one that abdicated the throne, visited the north east to see what we were grumbling about. He happened to be in Bishop Auckland and he was looking at the old church where the Jarrow marchers stayed. They

had then turned it into a social club for the unemployed, just to keep them off the street. I got a bit too near his car and the chauffeur got out and gave me a clip across the ear. When war started in 1939 it solved the unemployment problem, but that's another story.

Jake Bake

Leasingthorne School

We had slate boards to write on when I first went to school. The headmaster was Mr Bewick, he was the best headmaster in the district and taught me scripture, writing and everything. When I was seven I used to get the stick six times a day, for talking. I was a bit of a chatterbox. They were the good old days.

Mary Simpson

Open Day

We performed a maypole dance on open day. We had dresses made from blue and white crepe paper. Flossie Goundray made the dresses. I can still remember the song we sang.

Come let us cut the flax plant today
Heckle it first then spin, spin away.
Then shall we weave the curtail and skirt
Then twist and twine in dancing.
We can dance and we can sing
We can make a fairy ring.
We can wind the colours gay.
Children come the fairies call
Come, come, come, come
Come, come, come, come

St Wilfreds School,
Bishop Auckland.

(dunk six times)
Then twist and twine in dancing.

Mary Simpson

Prayers

Joan Thrower and Elsie Robinson used to play the piano on the way in for prayers. There was no teacher to play so the scholars used to do it.

Mary Simpson

Jumble Sale

When we were in Miss Walkers class, she was lovely and we would do anything for her, we had a jumble sale to buy a gramophone.

Mary Simpson

Horse Drawn

I am 74 and was born in Clayton Street, Bishop Auckland, behind what is now the bus station. Clayton Street ran into Hamburgh Square where the original fire station was. They kept the horse-drawn fire engine there. They also kept the fever van there, to take people with infectious diseases to the Isolation Hospital. As children we ran away when we saw the fever van because you thought you might catch something. Poverty was rife in Clayton Street, some of the houses were little more than hovels.

Catherine McGannon

17

McIntyres shoe shop is now Etam. The original frontage has been preserved behind the new facade.

Police Station

Our house in Clayton Street backed onto the old police station. They kept the police horses in a stable at the back. At night you could hear the police horses kicking the doors.

Catherine McGannon

Old Cattle Mart

The cattle mart used to be where Asda stands now. I remember cows being driven along the streets to the market.

Catherine McGannon

St Wilfreds School

I went to St Wilfreds school and we went to St Wilfreds church in Etherley Lane. I was always told that the stained glass windows in the church were St Andrew and St Helen because St Wilfreds grew out of the parish churches in the area. The stone cross that was on the church was moved when the church at Woodhouse Close was built.

Catherine McGannon

Benefactors

The glass plaques at the front of St Wilfreds church are dedicated to the McIntyre family, who had a shoe shop. They did a great deal of good in the town, especially for poor children. The teacher would give a child with no shoes a ticket and they would go to the shop and get some new shoes or boots. One of the McIntyre's sons was killed when the fair was in the market place. He was giving out tickets to poor children, to have a free ride on the roundabouts, when he fell into the machinery. He was only seventeen.

Catherine McGannon

School Milk

A man used to come to the school from the County Health Department. He used to stand in front of the class and look at all the children. We used to try to look pale and frail so he would chose us. He would point a finger and say 'that one' We hoped he was pointing at us, but it was always the one next to you. Those he chose got a free pint of milk a day and a biscuit. I think it was the biscuit that was the attraction. The rest of us used to have to take two h'pence a week for our milk.

Catherine McGannon

Canney Hill

I was born in 1913 in the village of Canney Hill, which is one mile from Bishop Auckland, on the main road leading to Durham. Most of the village, along with the adjacent village of Coundon Gate, was wiped out when Category D came into force. My father and grandfather were miners at Auckland Park Colliery. When I was a child there were many shops in the village. Starting at Crossways House, there was Mrs Burdess, a pork butcher. The cottage at the bottom of Grange Hill Lane was Mrs Denham's post office, their daughter Janet was the postwoman during the First World War and made deliveries on horseback.

A family called Goldsborough lived in a cottage known as Banty Cock Cottage, after the bantams they kept there. St Bernards House was called that because the Egglestone brothers who lived there kept St Bernard dogs.

The Black Boy Inn was converted into a dwelling house many years ago and was occupied by Mr James Lee, the headmaster of Coundon RC School. The cottage next door was a small shop run by an old lady called Mrs Dowson. The shop was really just the front room with a few boxes of fruit and the like.

The Sportsman Inn had a ball alley where hand ball was played against the end wall. The area was used as a car park until December 1996 when an extension was built over the area where the men used to play handball. Next was Canney Hill pottery. Near the pottery was the house of Mr Alf Roucroft who bought the land where the pottery had been and built a large garage. He set up a bus service with Mr W. Potts, called the Favourite Service, that ran from Bishop Auckland to Spennymoor, Ferryhill, Bishop Middleham, Stockton and Middlesbrough.

Young's hardware shop was at No. 10 and sold paraffin and groceries. They were Pentecostals and religious slogans were whitewashed on the shop windows and religious texts printed on the packets of salt, sugar and other things.

A boxing booth was set up at behind No. 9. The men used to crowd up the stairs there to see the fights.

Next door, at No. 8, a Working Men's Club was started, but it wasn't a success and the shareholders lost their money. The steward was Tommy Reed. Years later, when the loft was cleared out, they found boxes of membership cards.

There were three rows of two-roomed cottages, with pantries, in Bowman Terrace, Garden Terrace and Coundon View. They had cold water taps, gas (there was no electricity in the village),

Coundon Gate

Vera Bradford, née Gibbon, of Coundon. We see her in 1914, aged 7 months.

There were five streets in Coundon Gate. Park Avenue, facing the Bishops Park; Grange View, facing Grange Hill (these were always referred to as the new buildings as they were built between 1900 and 1910); Park View, Chapel Street and Spring Terrace. They were all demolished years ago. The end cottage on Spring Terrace was originally the gatehouse (hence Coundon Gate), it jutted out part of the way over the pavement and the gable end had a painted sign - McIntyres boot and shoe repairs. Mrs Holdsworth set up a small shop in the scullery of her home in Grange View. Later her and her family moved into Park Avenue and the sitting room became a shop on a large scale.

A family called Jackson lived in Park Avenue. Their sitting room was converted into a drapery shop, with a bay window display. On display were balls of Dolly Farthing Wool (variegated) - one penny each. I used these for cork knitting where you had an old cotton bobbin with nails in the end and knitted a long tail, which you stitched into things. The village post office was at No. 6 with a counter in the passage. The village bobby lived at No. 8. Miss Katy Greaves, who lived at No. 2, taught music at one shilling and three pence per lesson, or fifteen shillings per quarter.

Milk was delivered by Mr Rothery with a can and a measure. He put your milk in a jug that you took to the door. The Doctors Call House was in Spring Terrace and if you wanted a doctor to call you left a message. The doctor drove a pony and trap. If you

coal houses and earth closets, a few yards from the back doors. Most of the cottages had a framed slate on the wall near the door. The miners chalked up the time they wanted to be knocked up. So the village had a 'knocker up' who got paid for doing the job.

These cottages were on three sides of an area of ground with a stone wall on the fourth side. This was always referred to as the Square and every year a bonfire was lit on 5 November. Not many fireworks, just a few sparklers. Also in Bowman Terrace was a reading room where the men used to sit and chat and read the daily papers.

Vera Bradford

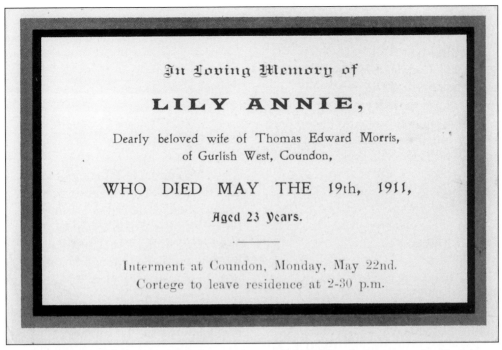

In Loving Memory of

LILY ANNIE,

Dearly beloved wife of Thomas Edward Morris,
of Gurlish West, Coundon,

WHO DIED MAY THE 19th, 1911,

Aged 23 Years.

———

Interment at Coundon, Monday, May 22nd.
Cortege to leave residence at 2-30 p.m.

Victorians made a great deal of death and funereal rites. Black edged cards were sent to friends and relatives to notify them of the death and of the timing of the funeral.

wanted a prescription he would leave it at the Call House from where you would collect it. All the streets were lit with gas lights. We had a lamp lighter - 'Anty' (Anthony) Johnson. He toured early on winter nights to light and late on winter mornings to put out.

There was a funeral bidder. This was someone who knocked on your door if anybody had died in the village. He said 'You are bidden to so and so's funeral, which is at the church or the chapel at such and such a time and afterwards.' This meant that there was a tea after the funeral and all were welcome. Two ladies in the village attended every funeral just to go to the tea. How people afforded it was amazing, but even at the poorest time a funeral was not complete without a tea being provided. When the funeral procession left the village

two women walked in front of the horse drawn hearse, each carrying a wreath. They walked all the way to Coundon with the mourners walking behind. Often there was a long procession of people walking to the churchyard.

My mother gave me my laying out clothes when I married and I have them in a chest upstairs. These were always ready so that when people called to see the deceased they would be presentable. The laying out clothes consist of a long white nightdress, white socks and a white pillow case. The trestles and boards for laying people out were kept in the village. They were collected and the person was put in the front room so that neighbours could come and pay their last respects.

Vera Bradford

Smithy

At the top of the lonnen [back lane], leading from New Coundon to Coundon, stood the smithy. Mr Hodgson was the blacksmith in about 1919. On the way home from school we used to call at the blacksmiths shop and watch Mr Hodgson at work.

Vera Bradford

A Tradgedy

The wood wagons used to travel through Coundon, Coundon Gate and Canney Hill carrying felled trees with their branches chopped off, probably from Wynyard or Windlestone Estates. They were fastened onto low loaders with heavy chains and were pulled by a team of heavy horses on their way to Wolsingham or Witton le Wear. A little girl called Annie Nesbitt, aged six, in the same class as me at school, was killed in 1919. During the school dinner break she ran after the wood wagon, jumped on for a ride, fell off and must have gone under the wheels. She is buried in Coundon churchyard.

Vera Bradford

Banning the Banns

My mother used to tell me about a time in St Wilfreds church when the banns of marriage were being read out. The bride's father did not approve of the groom and he stood up and said 'I forbid this marriage'. The priest said 'Shut up and sit down Martin Sweeney. I'll speak to you later.' The couple got married.

Catherine McGannon

Etherley Moor

I was brought up in Etherley Moor, in the 1930s, until I was six or seven, when we moved to Darlington on my birthday. I didn't want to go and I cried all the way. The house we lived in at Etherley Moor has gone now. I remember it had an earth floor downstairs and my father used to pull the oil lamp chandelier down to light it. My father had the first gramophone in the village, one in a big cabinet. I remember it coming on a horse and cart. My father left the front door open so that people could hear it.

I went to St Wilfreds School and we used to walk down Etherley Lane. We used to go to Fothergills fruit shop, next to the Masons Arms, to buy apples and bananas. Sometimes on our way to school we saw the steam wagons delivering beer to the Pollards Inn. I remember their screeching whistles. We used to go and see the village blacksmith, which was alongside the Miners Club. There was a drift mine opposite. We were having our teas one night and we all rushed out because this airship was going over. I remember it was black on the edges and gold across the middle, like a big kipper.

We once gave a concert from St Wilfreds in the town hall. I was dancing with big ears. All the proud parents sat in the front rows. The head teacher was Miss Weldon and there was Miss Cross.

Etherley Moor. Note the gas lighting.

I remember a chant we used to have when we were at school,

> Who's that coming down the street?
> Mrs Simpson, sweaty feet.
> She's been married twice before,
> Now she's knocking at the dukes back door.

I was sent to McIntyre's from school, for a new pair of boots because it was the time of the depression and nobody had any money.

John Conroy

Cockton Hill School

I was born in 1923 and went to Cockton Hill School. I know I got the cane a lot. I owe a lot to one of the teachers called Harry Thubron. He was in the First World War and had trench feet. He taught us as much as he could and I ended up winning a scholarship to King James Grammar School in 1934/35. There used to be a board in the school hall at Cockton Hill with the names of the pupils who had passed the scholarship. In those days you had to have an interview. This was held in the Friends Adult School, which was opposite Raines, the tobacconists in South Church Road. The first year classes were held in the Friends Adult School.

Donald Callender

The village of Etherley Moor is seen from Etherley Dene.

King James

I remember some of the teachers at King James School in 1935. There was 'Snitch' Hesleridge who taught English and Freddie Willie Yielder who taught maths. The headmaster was Mr Morrison who was a towering, fearsome person, but fair. We were taught Esperanto by Russell Hamilton, who played cricket for Bishop, but we were only taught it for one year.

Donald Callender

Motor Mechanic

My father was a sergeant pilot in the First World War, he worked in Vales Garage down Gibb Chare. He worked there from 1923 until the outbreak of the Second World War. One of the jobs he did was to maintain the town's police car, which was a Lagonda - a beautiful beast. He also mended machines for the Lingford Baking Powder Factory. Bert Vale and his wife, Lucy, lived in Craddock Villas.

Donald Callender

The Derby Hotel

I learned to play darts in the Derby Hotel in Tenters Street, because my aunt, Mary Callender, was the landlady there. She was a handsome woman and was my haven when I was in trouble at home. We lived just down the street. She was a widow, my Uncle Kit had been killed in the First World War. Behind the Derby were Hawthorne

24

Cottages, they were the most awful slums in the town. Just past there was a cattle yard and the slaughter house, past where the post office is now.

Donald Callender

The Farrs

I remember Farr's yard because we lived in Wood Street, which has gone now. The Farrs were old people who lived in a house in William Street with a housekeeper, who I called Aunty Polly Harrison. I remember being led up the stairs to the bedroom and the old couple were sitting up in bed with the Kings telegram. It was their Diamond Wedding.

At Christmas there was an area in Farr's Yard where they used to roast a sixteen-pound turkey every year.

Donald Callender

School Trips

We once went on a school trip to London, it cost a pound, which was a lot of money in those days. I think my mother must have saved it up. We formed up at Bishop Auckland railway station at midnight and went by train. I remember we went to Lyons Corner House and to London Zoo. We must have been hardy souls in those days. We also went on a school trip to Whitley Bay. I think the attraction was the Spanish City.

Donald Callender

Tindale Crescent

I was brought up in Tindale Crescent, next to the post office. My father worked for Shaw and Knight, the sanitary ware company, which stood near the railway bridge at Fylands. We used to play in a field where the factories now stand and I remember shows being where Elliots Motors used to be, which was opposite where they are now. I first went to school at St Helens, I remember we used to have to pass the graveyard and we ran past.

On Sundays we went to a little church at Fylands which has gone now. There used to be a big Dalmatian dog living in one of the houses on our way to church and we used to hurry past in case we got bitten. My grandfather kept a horse in a field near the river, past the church, and we used to go and see it.

I played whip and top on the pavement outside our house. There wasn't as much traffic then as there is now. We used to walk with my mother up the road to Etherley. We had a relative there and one at Toft Hill. I remember there used to be allotments on the corner next to the hospital.

Maureen Toner

Young Film Stars

We were chosen by the headmasters of various schools in Bishop Auckland to take part in a film, for local studies, about the town. The whole exercise was to give people in the town an insight into what was happening in Bishop. The camera team from the Ministry of Education came

The cast are seen here sitting on Brusselton Bank, at the beginning of filming. They are discussing the project with Donald Finlay, who played the part of George – the character who guides the children through their investigation into the town of Bishop Auckland.

round each school with Kay Mander, the director, and we had to read out of a book to hear what our voices were like. Appearances counted as well. I had been in various plays at school.

The whole project was held in an old chapel called The Friends and Adults Meeting Hall, in South Street. We went, every morning, to work on the project for about four weeks. No expense was spared, we had all the wood, pens and paper we wanted.

So that we could get on together they gave us a day, out on Brusselton, with Mr Richards, who played the sort of father figure in the film.

One of the jobs was the reading of the maps and we had to make a papier-mâché scale model of the area. We started with a sand tray, first drawing in the rivers. Then we tore up paper, soaked it in a bucket and made a ball which we used to make the shape of the hills. Betty Dakin and I thought it would be nice to show what we had done to friends and family and Mr Richards suggested we might hold an exhibition when we had finished. The whole team was then drawn in.

The scale maps we got from Bishop Auckland town hall. We had to interview people in high offices like the engineer and surveyor, Mr Ford.

We went to Wilson's Foundry - it was like the bowels of the earth. Little did I know then that I would become

Work on the relief map of Bishop Auckland, for use in the film Near Home, was taking place at this sand table.

an engineering pattern maker. We were then taken to see the Roman hypercaust under Mr Wedgewood's field at Vinovium. Then, you went through a trapdoor in the ground and had to weave your way around the pillars on your hands and knees. Now they have opened it all up.

I remember going to the farm (Grange Hill Farm) because I tore my corduroy jerkin there. I was messing about swinging on a hook. I got into trouble from the film makers for messing about and when I got home I got a telling off from my mother for tearing my jerkin.

They had a proper film crew, with lights, they would only film if the light was right. The film was shot in sections and sometimes we had to do things

over again. I remember one line I had to say, 'Look Mr Richards. I've found a very interesting book.' I couldn't get it right because, kid-like, I gabbled it. I had to say it a few times until they were satisfied, but in the end I got it right and it's in the film and in the book. On the big day of the exhibition, held in the old chapel in South Road, parents and people from the council were invited. They were asking questions and there was general interest.

Trevor Davies

[*The film was made by the Ministry of Education in 1948 to bring visual aids into the teaching of local studies in schools. Experience during the Second World War, using film in studies leading up to the use*

The House Where I Was Born

Trevor Davies was one of the stars of the film *Near Home*.

of the Mulberry Harbour, off the coast of France, after D-day, demonstrated the use of film as a teaching aid. The Bishop Auckland film, Near Home, was the first attempt to use this new medium.
The video of this film came back to Bishop Auckland quite by chance. Dr Ken Walton, a local man, was visiting Auckland Castle from Llanfairpwill in Wales (where he now lives and works as an honorary lecturer at the University of Wales). He happened to mention the existence of this long forgotten film and very kindly supplied a copy. The booklet, which accompanied the film, has been carefully preserved by Mrs Mildred Liddell of Durham Road, Bishop Auckland.]

I was born in 15a Fleet Street, in Cockton Hill. It was an end house, facing another end house, of one of the three blocks (and one short) that make up the street. We moved to 23 Fleet Street when I was quite small, less than five I think because I started school from No. 23 - Cockton Hill School, of course, only one block from our house. Ashcroft Gardens had not been built then. There was a field out our back, then Davidson's orchard and then the railway. Fleet Street seemed to be full of railwaymen in those days. Not as many as Dent Street in Tindale though, where the foreman, Alderman Bob Middlewood, lived surrounded by several of my father's brothers.

The main room was where we lived and we ate in the kitchen. Beyond that, towards the back, was the back kitchen where food was prepared and dishes washed - clothes as well on wet days. Clothes were washed in the yard on fine days. Almost nobody had the household appliances we take for granted nowadays, that make life easier and more comfortable. For example, we had no washing machine, no vacuum cleaner, no fridge or freezer and not even an immersion heater. I guess most of the houses were rented. I remember when I was quite small being alarmed at the rent collector, who used to knock and enter without being asked in. I sometimes had to take the rent, fourteen shillings a week, up to the landlord, Tommy Parkin. He had a butcher's shop on the main road.

The road outside was unmade. There was a flagged pavement and a gutter,

We see here the exhibition which took place after *Near Home* was completed.

but the rest of the space between the blocks of houses was made up of stones embedded in dirt. Because all the houses were heated with open coal fires, the term 'dirt' really meant just that. When it rained the road turned into a black, slimy mess, with deep puddles glittering here and there. The backs of the houses were worse. Each back gate opened into a back lane where the surface was made up of dirt and cinders.

Ken Walton

A Technological Advance

At the second house we had a washing machine, but one that you would scarcely recognise today. Then it was a great advance in technology. A large metal body on four wooden legs held the water. Inside was a cylindrical wooden cage with solid ends, this came into two halves so that you could put the clothes inside. The cylinder was rotated in the hot water by means of a shaft that ran through its centre to a wheel outside the metal case and was driven by hand-operated wooden lever, crank and gears. When we used it during my teens, my brother-in-law and I used to give it 'forty each way' and then stop for a smoke. The clothes were then put through the other part of the machine, a mangle with unevenly worn wooden rollers. When the clothes were nearly dry, no mean feat in bad weather, they were ironed with another innovation - an electric iron. Unfortunately, it had no thermostat to control the temperature, so keeping an even heat was guesswork.

Ken Walton

Workers at LNER West Auckland Depot (Tindale), *c.* 1920. Pictured on the back row are, Harry Walton, Walter Walton and Billy Walton (extreme right). These three were brothers in a family of fourteen children. Their parents were Thomas and Ester Walton of 15 Dent Street, Bishop Auckland. Two other sons were railwaymen as well as their father, Thomas.

Cockton Hill School

My mother tried to get me into Cockton Hill School when I was only four years old, in September 1936, but they weren't having any. When I look back at my old school reports I can see one very good reason - some classes had fifty children in them! I finally started, just after my fifth birthday, in the infants class with Miss Bell, she was plump, spectacled and kind. You got rides in the swing with ducks on the side, or the rocking horse, if you behaved yourself and did well at reading. Tommy [Tommy Greenhaulgh] and I were good at reading, it was something we just took to. We moved up the infant classes to junior school - Miss Hamphlet, Miss Scott,

Miss Worden (a World War started somewhere about here). The school was run by Miss Patterson, also plump and spectacled. She usually played the piano for prayers, some stirring march to get the troops into position.

My only outstanding memory from this school, apart from the coronation of George VI and Elizabeth Bowes-Lyon, in May 1937, was taking part in a play about Robin Hood. I was cast as Richard the Lionheart, resplendent in chain-mail armour (LNER cleaning cloths in thick cotton weave) and a shining sword put together by my father and painted silver with aluminium paint.

Ken Walton

Andrew Morrison, headmaster of King James I Grammar School, is seen here with the school football team on 15 June 1943.

A Scholarship Boy

I started King James Grammar School in the autumn of 1943, having just passed the scholarship, the forerunner to the 11 plus, in the summer. Before the war it had been a proper exam in English and maths but the risk of having exams interrupted by air raids had forced the county council to change its form. The exam I did was a paper consisting entirely of intelligence questions to be answered in a short fixed time, probably an hour. We found out what sort of gear we needed for the new school - a cap and a tie in the school colours, maroon and gold. The tie was striped, the cap carried the school device and what I thought was a motto but turned out to be Schola Regis Aucklandensis which simply means The Royal School of Auckland. Not a real match for our companion Bishop Auckland Girls Grammar School (whose name, unfortunately, abbreviated to BAGGS) which was Non sibi sed alis, mistranslated as 'not Sybil but Alice'. It was only when I got to the school that I found we had a proper motto - Laborare est orare, meaning to work is to pray.

The school was divided, as well as classes, by houses. There were four of these, named after the eponymous king and the three benefactors who, in 1605, had made possible the foundation of the school, originally housed in a building in the market place, hence King's, Swyft's, Morton and Neale's. I enjoyed most of the subjects we had to study, although the teachers were a very mixed bunch. Many of the former staff were either serving in the armed forces or engaged in war work of some kind. The ones that were left were either past the age of call up, or had been exempted for some other reason.

My third and subsequent years found

31

me in the main part of the school, in our own classroom, which we left from time to time for particular classes in other rooms, such as the one reserved for geography, the laboratories, or the library.

I always liked the library. It was virtually the only room in the school that looked like the sort of place you see in movies with schools in them. It was in the oldest part of the building and had a solid wooden door with wrought iron handles. Beyond the door was a long narrow room lined with bookshelves, on the right, and a big old-fashioned fireplace on the left. The centre of the room was taken up by a polished wooden table, its grain reflecting the light from the big bay window at the end opposite the door. The window faced south across the headmaster's lawn to the playing fields beyond and so on, to the adjacent girl's school. The table was well supplied with round-backed, wooden armchairs.

In the February of my final year, 1950, our headmaster, Andrew Morrison, retired. He had run the school since the autumn of 1928, so that an entire generation of boys had known no other. I find myself unable to assess whether or not he was a good head, never having known another - except his successor, for a very short time. He put the fear of God into most pupils, but he was always understanding and helpful when you needed it. I remember him with genuine affection.

Ken Walton

The Dancing Master

An account of these years would be incomplete without saying something about dancing classes, which started in the 4th form. By this time I could just keep my feet in the right place for the waltz, having once been graciously but firmly lured to my feet by Betty, one of the two Warren girls whose father ran an electrical supply shop near the Hippodrome. Some of my classmates already knew how to dance after a fashion. These were the 'men about town' who frequented Spennymoor Rink on a Saturday night. It was the nearest dance hall to Bishop.

Bob Soulsby normally taught English, but was prepared to spend his own free time coaching us in this, in his view, essential social accomplishment. And it meant we got to meet girls. They were allowed to come down from their own school, after lessons, one afternoon a week and join us to be coached in the elements of the quickstep, the modern and old-fashioned waltzes, the valeta and the military two-step, to the music of records played by a loudspeaker. The event took place in the old gym, part of the old building, past the library and beneath the science labs. It still had fittings from the time it had been the only gym, before the new one was built at the edge of the grounds.

Ken Walton

Further Education

When you left school you either got a job or could continue your education at the tech. I went to

Pupils of Newfield Junior School, in 1949.

the tech in 1956 for full time further education, learning English and maths. The main tech was at Station Approach, Bishop Auckland, which became the driving test centre and has now gone. The drawing office was a prefab. That was the building trades area around there. All the female side was above Burton's shop, for typing, and the metal works were along by the Green Tree. The machinery for testing stress on metals - metalurgy, was in the crypt of an old church up Tenters Street. How they got all the machinery down there I can't imagine. You went to another prefab at Cabin Gate, which was the canteen.

One of the instructors was called Hank Saunders, he was a cricketer. I went to Marshal Richards, at Crook, as an apprentice for five years and went back to the tech on day release. We were some of the first in the new building, in Woodhouse Lane, before the official opening. They had to redecorate the place because of the damage done by some of the apprentices from Shildon shops before they could open it.

There were no swimming baths in Bishop and we went on the bus to Darlington. You used to come back with your eyes streaming because of the chlorine in the water.

Brian Willis

CHAPTER 2

Trade and tradespeople

Bishop Auckland market place is seen here prior to the building of the town hall in 1862. This view shows St Annes church and the Butter Cross.

Bishop Auckland market place on market day.

Bishop Auckland Market

Many aspects of life in the market have long since been forgotten. The horse cabs of Hulls, the two wheeled barrow of Tommy Mutton - who used it to transport travellers samples from the station to the shops and then to the hotels where the travellers were staying. There would be pies and peas for a snack and the hot roast potato stalls, not all for eating but some for warming the lady's hands inside her muff. The South Shields fish wives brought their baskets of fresh fish and boiled shell fish by the first train in the morning and left by the first train after they had sold out. Then there were the regulars - Gill's pot stall, 'If you don't buy them I'll smash them', and he did (only those already damaged), Charlie Swales wet fish stall beside St Annes church (he looked well on it). Bradley & Harlands were

fruiterers, and as rosy as their apples, Hartley and Jones, the florist, Arkless for Ingersol watches. The butchery and dairy produce was in the ground floor of the town hall. Around the edges of the market there were still traces of the original farm and horticultural goods, tools and plants and even, until recently, hiring of farm workers.

We certainly shouldn't forget the band of the Salvation Army, who regaled us with Christmas carols, and Allswop, the match seller, with his wares on a small tray. He was an ex-railway worker, in ill health, but kindly and good mannered, he varied his pitch with the weather.

The blackout of World War Two brought to an end the activities carrying on after 10p.m. on Saturdays, when the light and heat was provided by hissing naphtha lamps. No longer able to do the last minute shopping when the pubs had closed and maybe get a bargain.

The well remembered Rossis Café stood opposite Theatre Corner in Bishop Auckland. The café was demolished in 1984.

After all hope of trading had gone, the stalls were cleared and the refuse removed ready for Sunday morning church parades, when new clothes were paraded and lingering gossips held sway after the crowded church services [at St Annes].

Frank Hutchinson 1985

[Frank gave the author his treatise on the history of the town before he died, in the hope that his work might one day be published. It seems appropriate to include some of it here.]

Fair Time

The focal point of the town was the market place with its variety of vendors, coconut shies, roundabouts and mysterious side shows crowding each other. Travelling zoos by Bostock and Wombwell, roundabouts by Richardsons, Murphy, Headley and Newsome. It was truly a town centre where the town met, rich and poor alike, shoulder to shoulder. The place was cleared of jam jars by the youngsters, in their efforts to get a few coppers to spend at the fair. Hanratty's [scrap merchants] was full of jars.

Frank Hutchinson 1985

Market Day

The market was always full of stalls. I remember the smell of the spring flowers especially mimosa, daffodils, and narcissus from the Channel Isles. Fresh eggs, farm butter and curds sold by Mr Denham. Hulls Tea Hut, Seatons toffee stall, Frazer materials, Webbs sweet stall - with liquorice allsorts at three pence a quarter. The wet fish stalls were Swales (Bishop Auckland), Hanselmanns (Spennymoor) and Taylors (Whitley Bay). On Saturday nights, about nine o'clock, they knocked the prices down. They shouted each other down until the prices were at rock bottom.

Around 1946 there was a tripe stall outside St Annes. Early on a Saturday morning there was always a queue. You were each allowed half a pound of tripe and half a pound of dripping. The lady who ran it came from Darlington. There was a stall at the corner of Bondgate selling fresh eggs, rabbits, fruit and flowers. I used to take eggs from our chickens and he gave me one shilling for thirteen eggs.

There were offices around the market place. Braithwaites, the printers and stationers, Doggarts Arcade, Jennings the solicitor, St Peters Vicarage (Revd Parry Evans), Proud, a solicitor, Loft, a solicitor and Roddam, a solicitor. The Mount School, a private school, Sibbald, seed merchant, Pratt, saddler (later Wade), Armstrong, undertaker. Norman Armstrong became the undertaker for the Co-operative Society. Gillettes, tyres (Wear Chare) and the United Bus Company offices.

Vera Bradford

Bondgate

In Bondgate was Miss Stubbs, dressmaker, Snaithe, tobacconist, Miss Daisy Snaith, needlework, Phillips, pianos, Tommy Stubbs, decorators, Hurworths, bakers and Storeys, bakers. There was also Vardys, fish and chips with seating accommodation upstairs (fish and chips were sixpence a plate), Mrs Patterson, tearooms, Crawfords pet food store and Mrs Hamilton, herbalist.

Vera Bradford

Property Bondgate and Market Place

One of my ancestors, Cuthbert Morson, a joiner, owned property in Bishop Auckland in 1866. I have a deed which shows that he owned 'the public house known by the sign of the Kings Arms' that is now called the Post Chaise, which had a joiners shop at the back. There was also six cottages behind the public house and a slaughter house and a stable.

He also owned a public house in Back Bondgate 'known by the sign of the Dun Cow' which had a brew house and a hayloft. It must have been very small because it consisted of 'one low room with a chamber over'. The property also had the rights to a pew in St Annes church.

George Morson

Roast Ox

I remember being taken when I was little, in the 1930s, to the fair in the market place in Bishop Auckland and there was a man roasting an ox over

Jimmy Shields enjoys a drink in the Sun Inn in Bishop Auckland, *c*. 1950. The premises were demolished, but the Sun Inn lives on in the Beamish Museum where drinks are still served to visitors.

a fire. He had a big ladle and he kept pouring this stuff over the ox on a spit on a fire. The smell was lovely, you could smell it all over Bishop. My father bought some, just a little piece because it was very expensive.

John Conroy

Rossis

There was Rossis ice cream and coffee shop, which was the meeting place for all the young blades and teenage girls. It was easy to make one cup of coffee last a long time. There was never any trouble that I remember. The shop was later transferred to the market place where it is still very popular. [It has now closed.]

Marjorie Graham

Cheap Meals

There was a British restaurant in Farr's Yard, Bishop Auckland in 1931. It was set up so that people could get a cheap meal, because times were hard in the area and the people did not have enough money to buy a good dinner.

Marjorie Graham

Travelling People

My family has lived in Bishop Auckland for generations and were all travelling people. My grandfather, Jimmy Shields, was a trader in the town and my mam's side were all original gypsies, called Romany travellers, living in horse-drawn caravans called living wagons. My mother's maiden name was O'Neil and she had always lived in a living wagon. The children were born in the wagons.

In the winter they would rent a house, as it was easier for the children. In a bad winter they just had a stove. The wagons had a wooden frame with canvas stretched over it. They would build a wooden frame on a four-wheeled wagon, the work was unbelievable, all carved and painted with gold.

The first time me mam lived in a house was when she got married, when she was twenty-six. Later on families progressed with time and got cars and lived in modern caravans, which were all chrome. Her dad died when she was six and as her brothers got older they took over the man's role.

My grandfather had a fruit and vegetable business in High Tenters Street and me dad worked for him after school. He left school pretty early, then they were out rag and boning, what you called 'old stuffing', iron, heavy iron, rags. They would sort the rags out, the woollens from the others, because woollens brought a better price. You used to take an old quilt and bundle the corner full of woollens and sort them from what they called 'the tats'. We used to go out tatting and take them to the scrap yard. There are not many left but there was one in Blackett Street. After you left school you went round to 'hawk', which means you went round the streets. You would go here and you would go there. With the fruit and vegetables you went round shouting.

They would buy ponies and horses, which they would sell for extra money. When they came back they would give the head of the house the money, he would give them so much back. In them

days it was a couple of pound. They didn't work for themselves until they were married. While they were at home it was a family commitment where everybody chipped in. That made it a lot easier because if one had a bad week it made no difference because everybody got the same. The family stuck together, with the head of the household having the say, whether it was the father or the mother, until the sons were old enough to take on the man's role.

Eddie Shields

Appleby Fair

My grandfather bought a lot of ex-pit ponies which he used to take to Appleby to sell. He travelled on a flat cart with a sort of tent on the top, not a four-wheeled living wagon. Now it would take an hour - then it would take a week for the journey. You can only go so far with a horse in a day because it gets tired. Sometimes they would set off maybe a fortnight earlier and go so many miles a day then they would stop, give the horses a rest. Now it's all changed and you're not allowed to stop on the side of the road. They would go ten or fifteen miles a day, tie up the horses and then move on.

You were on the road and you lived on the road because if you lived in a house you looked forward to it. It was a sort of holiday, it used to bring back memories of the old times and they used to talk of the different times they went to Appleby.

Years ago the men used to go to the fair and the women used to stop in the camp. The men used to go and do the

Frankie Shields proudly shows off one of his fine horses at the end of Fore Bondgate in Bishop Auckland.

business. Running the horses up the street so that people could see them and if you saw a horse you liked you stepped out and asked how much.

It's all changed now, they put the carts on low loaders and many just hire them for a show. In the old days it was a chance to meet people who you didn't see from one year to the next.

Eddie Shields

The Women

On me mam's side of the family the women would go out to work. They would go out and they would tell fortunes. Me granny did in Bishop Auckland. She told fortunes out of a house she lived in at the top of Newton Cap Bank, her name was Isobel O'Neil. In the olden days, her and me mam used to walk from where they were camping, maybe five or six miles, to a little village where they would sell lucky charms. They would knock on the doors and tell fortunes and sell locks of heather, things like that, and clothes pegs. That was their contribution to the home. When they were on the road they had to do as much as the men did.

My granny used to tell fortunes with a crystal ball, she sometimes used cards and sometimes tea leaves but she liked the crystal ball. She had women and men who used to come regular. The women would do whatever they could to keep the family together, everyone put their own bit in.

Eddie Shields

Marriage

Our families tended to marry people from similar families, with similar backgrounds. Sometimes they met at the dance, which was held at Appleby at fair time when the travelling people got together for an evening. The old people sat around talking of old times and the younger ones had a good time and got to know people from other families, but not getting drunk like they do now with cans of lager. Travelling people are very close, they stick together as a family and keep themselves to themselves.

Eddie Shields

The End Of The Road

When my grandfather died they burnt his wagons. They sometimes burnt their possessions as well. They kept the bits off the wagons that were needed for the family, like the springs and the corner plates, which were often very elaborate. If you had money the corner plates were made of brass, all hand made, all fancy and engraved - they were often passed on through generations.

Eddie Shields

Trading

The Maid of Erin pub in West Road, Bishop Auckland used to be the place where the horse traders used to meet. They stood outside, showed off their horses and struck bargains.

There is one story of a trader who had a particularly good horse to sell and his wife sent their young grandson to mingle with the crowd outside the Maid of Erin to see how much his grandfather got for the horse. When the grandfather got home he told his wife he had got fifteen pounds whereas he had got twenty-five pounds. She being well known as a clairvoyant pretended to know otherwise through the medium of her deceased mother. The husband paid up. The Maid of Erin is now a house but you can still see the trapdoor under the window, where the beer barrels were rolled into the cellar.

Betty Brown

Coalmen

Coal fires were pretty much the norm in my young days. The coal was delivered to our homes by coal wagon. The coal merchant would empty the sack of coal and then throw the sack onto the ground. The children watching would be instructed to count the sacks, and then inform their mothers if they were short (children were better at maths then). There were suggestions that coal merchants cheated a little by concealing one sack on a shoulder and throwing this, with the genuine sack, to the ground. I do remember one grocer who used to wash his currents and sultanas so they weighed heavy.

Marjorie Graham

The Vart family ran a painting and decorating business. Standing to the left is Paul Vart, his nephew, Harry Vart, is also standing.

Service

A lot of goods were delivered then. There was a Co-op bakery van and there was a fruit cart, a wet fish cart, a laundry van and of course the Ringtons tea van. My mother would give her order to the assistant from Brough's grocery store on Wednesday and it would be delivered all neatly packed. I call that service.

Amy Hodgson

Painting and Decorating

My grandfather was in the painting and decorating business as Vart & Bellerby and he played the violin in Nicholas Kilburns orchestra. The slogan of the business was 'What's in a name. Art is in Vart.' This was shown on the fire screen at the theatre.

Amy Hodgson

Shopping

We did our shopping in Bishop when we lived at Etherley, but everybody came round the Store [the Co-op] every fortnight. One week the order man came, the suits were put on the list, that's how they got their new suits. The Store had a big suit department - bespoke tailoring. He came round to the house and you paid your bill at the shop. We had a big list and we used to rhyme them off. They called him Mr Wales. They had a big wagon to deliver them. The Co-op baker van was horse-drawn. Every Easter you had to have a new hat or it was unlucky.

Amy Hodgson

Ice Cream

Di Palamas ice cream was a great favourite, especially on hot summer days. There was a boy on a bicycle who sold Eldorado, a form of fruit sorbet, which some how never caught on, although I really liked it.

Marjorie Graham

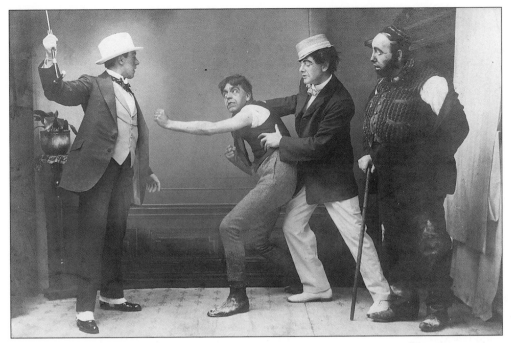

The man in the white trilby is Jack Vart (the opera singer), the brother of Fred and Paul Vart of the Bishop Auckland decorating family.

Good For Roses

There was still a few horses and carts about when I was a girl, and people with gardens would come out when they heard horses hooves in the hope of catching some manure for their plants.

Marjorie Graham

Rag and Bone Man

The rag and bone man used to give you a scoury stone, for scouring steps and hearths, in return for a small amount of rags and a goldfish for a large amount.

Vera Bradford

Collectable

Patterns, such as birds and flowers or your name, were put on the pottery made at Canney Hill, using paper cut outs, stuck to the pots before the final glaze was put on and then removed before firing. Dealers went round the village a few years ago buying up any pots that people in the village had, as Canney Hill pottery had become collectors items.

Vera Bradford

Shards

The girls in the village used the broken pieces of pot, from behind where the pottery used to be, to play a game, which involved throwing them onto numbered squares. These pieces were very hard and sharp and one girl lost her eye when a piece hit her. After the pottery closed we used to play in the field and make butter pats from the clay, like we saw the man in the grocers shop doing.

Vera Bradford

[The outcropping of thick clays at Canney Hill gave rise to a pottery industry, beginning in the nineteenth century. The three small companies engaged in the industry were Coopers, Bell Bros and Kay & Greaves. The oldest of the three companies was Coopers, who specialised in the making of 'stoneware', for instance stone bottles and jam jars, all having stone coloured outsides and white insides. The second business, Bell Bros, began soon after the first and specialised in 'yellow ware' - teapots, side dishes and similar. The latest pottery company was Kay & Greaves. They made more refined things with brown outsides and white insides - like cooking dishes, basins and jugs.

It was because of the exhaustion of the local clay that the industry declined and finally ended. Very primitive methods and machinery were employed in production, involving mostly manual labour. The prepared clay was thrown on a potters wheel, driven by a girl who varied the speed of the wheel as required by the potter. The finished article was then put into a drying room in which old-fashioned flues ran throughout. During drying there was always a peculiar smell.

Altogether, ten or twelve men would be employed by each company, so that no more than thirty-six men would be employed at any one time.]

A Family Business

My great grandfather, Thomas Bellerby, was a native of Witton le Wear but was brought to Bishop

Auckland at the age of two. He was an only son and his mother was widowed when he was nine years of age, his father being killed in an accident at Randolph Colliery. He was practically self taught in the art of painting and received his education from the Barrington school.

He was a great reader and a keen student of men and affairs. Later in life he took an active part in the old time Debating Society in Bishop Auckland. At the early age of twenty-one he began a business, going into partnership with Mr Harry Vart in 1881 as painters and decorators. About the beginning of the century the partnership was dissolved and Mr Bellerby continued on his own account. His personal tastes, however lay in landscape and portrait painting and he organised, and exhibited at, the first art exhibition held in Bishop Auckland that was opened by Bishop Moule in 1913. His work was also on view at other local exhibitions and he took a delight in presenting portrait paintings to friends in the district.

Mr Bellerby was a member of the old Field Club of Bishop Auckland and was an active spirit in the effort to gain a museum for the town, but the scheme never came to fruition. He was a loyal supporter of the Baptist church.

Mr Bellerby died in 1939 and was survived by his wife, two sons and two married daughters. His two sons, Thomas and John Angus Bellerby were associated with him in the business. John saw to the running of the shop and staff and Thomas saw to the painters and decorators and outside work. Thomas won the Military Medal and Bar as a sergeant signaller in the Battle of the Somme. John trained as an engineer before he entered the family firm.

The shop was in premises in Newgate Street from 1906. It was then sold to

Above: John Dowson, boot and shoe maker of West Auckland, c. 1890.
Above Right: A portrait of Pricilla Dowson, wife of John Dowson.

another firm but Thomas B. Bellerby & Sons continued at a new address in Adelaide Street, Bishop Auckland. The business traded for sixty years as a high class decorator and paint supplier.

Ann Wood

Boot and Shoe Maker

My grandfather, John Dowson, was apprenticed to a bootmaker in Lartington, near Barnard Castle. He set up his own business in West Auckland. He used to walk to Bishop Auckland, to McIntyres, to buy his leather. When my mother was a little girl she often used to go with him and on a cold day he would buy her a roast potato to keep her hands warm when they were walking back.

Vera Bradford

Ironing

I worked at the Lily Laundry, just off Cockton Hill Road, for fifteen years as an ironer and presser. I used to walk from Coundon, where I lived, every day and we worked from 8.30a.m. to 5p.m. We didn't get much money but we were a happy lot. We worked round a big table and we used to chatter a lot. Matty Manners and his brother used to sit and watch us working to make sure we didn't stop. Old man McNaughton

Above: George Dowson, with young passengers, in 1913.

Above Right: William Dowson of Fylands, with his young cousin Robert Scott, sometime before 1912.

was the boss then. We did our work alright.

I remember there was some horse racing on and we weren't allowed to talk about it, but the dry cleaner gave us the name of a horse on the quiet, and it came in third.

The worst job was ironing the Bishop's coat sleeves, they were thick and wet and the iron would go dry and we had to come back and finish them off. Pre-war, one man worker courted a girl out of the factory and then they were married. Happy days. We worked for nine pence an hour. We didn't have a proper dining room, we used to sit outside where we could.

Ada Orton

West Auckland Brewery

The West Auckland brewery was founded in 1837. My grandfather, Alfred Monk, was born in 1881. The brewery went bankrupt and a group of local businessmen, which included Mr Whitfield, who owned the bone mill on Bone Mill Bank at South Church, put money into the brewery and my grandfather became Company Secretary. My father, Sidney Monk, took over as Managing Director in about 1910. He went to the First World War and his sister ran the brewery while he was away. When he came back he took over again and ran it until it was sold to Camerons, in 1957. In the 1930s the brewery bought the house and buildings

Above: Louisa Firby, seen here with her younger brother, *c.* 1920. They were cousins of Vera Bradford.
Above Right: Louisa Studholm was another cousin. She is pictured here with her dog.

from the Eden family, who had lived there before they moved to Windlestone Hall. My father died in 1976 at the age of ninety-three. Next to the Brewery Houses, where we lived, was a row of four cottages, which were for the brewery workers. In the first house lived the hind [farm labourer] from the farm behind the brewery. The next two had people who worked in the brewery and in the last one was Bob Smith who was the cooper.

Peter Monk

Sporting Prints

My mother was Patricia Cummins of the well known fishing tackle and printing business in Newgate Street, Bishop Auckland. They were a great golfing family and were prominent members of the Bishop Auckland Golf Club. There is still a competition held at the club for the Cummins Cup. The shop was about where Boots is now and the printing works were at the back.

Peter Monk

The offices of Shaw & Knight, sanitary suppliers of Tindale Crescent, are pictured here in the 1930s.

House to House

My father opened the Kings Hall Cinema on Newgate Street in 1913. When it opened the new seats had not arrived so the first patrons sat on wooden planks.

There was a cinema in Byers Green and it was my job to bring the cans of film, which had been used for their first house, to Bishop Auckland for showing at the second house at the Kings Hall. I travelled by train and one dark night the train stopped outside the station at Bishop and I jumped out. I fell heavily onto the track and although I didn't hurt myself the cans of film burst open and the film rolled out and spread all over. As you can imagine my father was not too pleased.

G. Rudd

Echoing Footsteps

The newspaper office for the *Northern Echo*, *The Evening Despatch* and *The Auckland Chronicle* was above the shops at the corner of Chester Street, Bishop Auckland. Five reporters and a photographer covered Bishop Auckland District and often worked late, covering evening meetings. The reports for *The Evening Despatch* had to be written up that night and put into what was known as the late parcel, a jiffy bag marked 'News Intelligence'. This was taken to the railway station late at night, through the old entrance, across the deserted platform and up the stairs into the signal box, where it was handed to the signalman to be put on the last train to Darlington. The parcel was collected at Darlington Station and rushed to the newspaper office for setting overnight. Little did readers realise, as they opened their evening papers the next day, that the news had been carried through the spooky silence of Bishop Auckland railway station, lit only by dim gaslights, by a reporter late at night with only echoing footsteps for company.

Marie Land

CHAPTER 3

Mining and miners

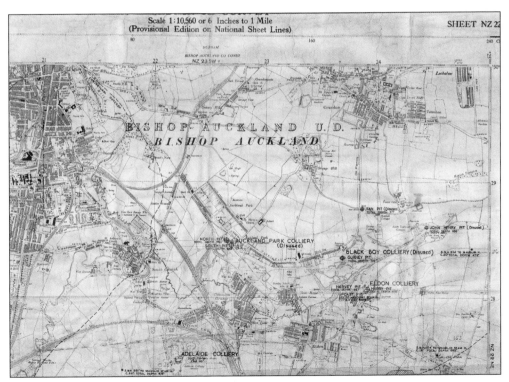

A Bishop Auckland Urban District Council plan of the coal mines in the Auckland Park area of 1954, showing the disused mines.

George Morson, now retired from the Coal Board, checks the water level in one of the capped shafts he was responsible for during his working life. He looked after the pumps that kept the water in the disused mines at an acceptable level.

Shafts In The Area

I worked for the NCB as a joiner, maintaining the pit shafts. We had to climb down into the shaft to replace much of the old woodwork, which was rotting, to stop the shaft caving in. We also had to make certain that the caps on the disused shafts were safe, as many of them are hundreds of feet deep and people might fall in. If there was still a working engineman, I had a certificate, as a shaftsman, allowing me to give the raps to signal to the engineman. The number of raps meant different things and there was often a board underground numbered up to thirteen raps. The last one was 'kenna' which was knocking off time. If there wasn't an engineman we had a metal

plate, hung on a string, which you hit with a hammer to give the raps to the bank [surface] so that the man on the top knew what was happening down below.

When we worked in a shaft we had a safety harness built into a jacket like a pilot's harness. If you fell, the stitches ripped out of the back of the jacket and a rope unwound, which was fastened to a holdfast in the shaft wall, to stop you falling to the bottom of the shaft - hundreds of feet below. Shafts move with the earth moving and sometimes there was a space between the cage and the wall. You had to be careful not to drop your stuff down there. One of the pits we worked in was Glebe Pit, near St Helens. This was one of the old pits where there was a shaft, which was divided into two

Form P. 39A

National Coal Board

Mines & Quarries Act, 1954.

Certificate of Authority as a Competent or Authorised Person.

No.

~~ Richmond Park Colliery

G. Morson is hereby

authorised to *operate electrical Switches and Shaft Signals and to perform all duties relating to that of "SHAFTSMAN"*

in accordance with the requirements of the Mines & Quarries Act, 1954 and the General Regulations and Orders made thereunder.

(Signed) Manager.

I hereby accept this authorisation and undertake to perform the duties and comply with the requirements prescribed by the Mines & Quarries Act, 1954 and the General Regulations and Orders made thereunder.

Date *8/2/67* Signature *G. Morson*

Permission to act as a shaft man. This would allow the holder to operate the shaft signals to the surface, calling for the operation of the cage to and from the mine.

by a wooden wall. On one side the coal came up and on the other there were ladders, which the miners had to climb down to get to the bottom. Every so often there was a platform with a square hole at one side to get to the next ladder. We had to climb down to repair the platforms and the timbers.

George Morson

Wet Money

You got different pay for working down the pit or at the bank. Eight hours at the bank or six hours down the mine. You got extra for working wet, but you didn't get it for just getting your feet wet, even though you might be working standing in a foot of water. You only got it for top water, that is water seeping through the roof. Mines can be very wet places.

George Morson

Hot and Cold

There is a lot of draught down a pit because of the ventilation. The down draught is very cold and the up draft is warm. Between ways there are cross tunnels with 'bratices', a sort of airlock made by two doors made of waterproof bratice cloth. You had to push hard on a door to get into the other way. Bratices were also used as temporary screens to keep dust down. We used to make the frames.

George Morson

53

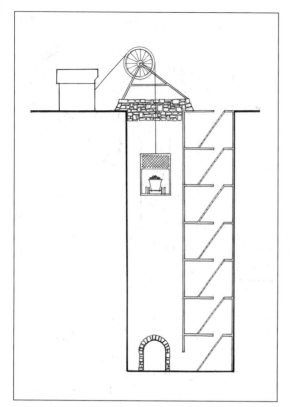

Above Right: The shaft of Glebe Pit, which was behind the school at West Auckland, was unusual in that it was divided by a wooden wall and accessed by ladders.
Above: Miners from Vinovium Pit are seen here early in the century.

Yard Sticks

One job I did was to make yard sticks for measuring the amount of work the miners did. They worked on what were called bargains, a sort of contract to hew a certain amount of coal. I made yard sticks out of old billiard cues, every miners hall and village hall had a billiard table in those days. I put brass nails every six inches so they could measure the seam.

George Morson

Talleys

We used to make talleys which were put into the tubs so that the check weighman at the bank could see who had hewed that tub of coal. The talleys were made of metal, with a string through a hole. There was a hole in the tub with a metal peg outside to fasten the string to. The talley was pushed through the hole into the tub before the coal was put in so that nobody could interfere with it until the tub was emptied. The check weighman, who was employed by the miners and not by the Coal Board, then hung the talley on a board so that when a miner came off

A coal miner, at the turn of the century, equipped for his shift with lamp and pick. He is wearing 'hoggars' - shorts made of coarse linen, worn by miners down the pit. Note the pick with its changeable head. This was developed to avoid having to sharpen the points, which soon became blunt. Miners usually carried a number of heads and sharpened them between shifts. Coal cutting machines replaced hand hewing except in very low seams.

All that remains of the West Auckland Colliery is this store house. The shaft was filled in some years ago.

Explosives were stored in the powder house, from where they were taken to the mines in the Coundon and Auckland Park area. No iron was allowed in the building, even the nails in the beams and the floor boards were made of copper. Note the blast wall erected on the east side.

shift he could see how much he was entitled to. The greatest crime in any pit was changing talleys.

George Morson

Broken Back Pit

This was at St Helens, where the factories are now It was called Broken Back Pit because so many miners injured themselves down there. My grandfather broke his back working there and lay for six years before he died. Conditions were not like they are now. They built the button factory over the shaft but they had to pull it down again because water used to seep up from the pit. The pit heap used to come right down to the wall, which is still there.

Sonny Dowthwaite

The Gallowa Putter

When I left school I got a job at Town End Drift at West Auckland. I got into trouble for galloping a pit pony. We used to collect the ponies at the beginning of the shift from Gaugers Arms Drift, up Toft Hill Road and ride them down to the drift, which was between St Helens and West Auckland. We used to take timber on a high-sided tub down to the face. At the end of the shift we used to ride the ponies back to the Gaugers Arms Drift,

This warning notice was supplied by the Imperial Chemical Company to advise of the penalties that would be incurred for causing an explosion in the magazine. It warns of immediate arrest, without a warrant, and a fine of fifty pounds.

Toronto pit lads, *c.* 1920. Harold Vart is on the front row, to the right.

This is a memorial to Durham miners in Durham Cathedral.

where they were stable behind the pub. The job was called a Gallawa Putter.

John Heighington

Sick Miners

Durham was still a coal mining area with pits at places like Newton Cap. I nursed some of the miners when I was a young nurse and I found many of them incredibly superstitious, although they were also very polite and thankful.

Marjorie Graham

Explosives

The powder house was where they stored powder for the mines. Mr Alf Roucroft, who went into partnership with Mr Potts at the garage, worked there. The powder was in long boxes, he used to deliver out to collieries and quarries. He used to travel up and down with a little van. Norman Arness used to be allowed to look round the powder house when he was a boy, but they had to take their boots off before they went in. There was a wooden floor, which was highly polished and a sign outside from ICI about looking after explosives, it was an enamel sign with ICI on it. The powder house was up a lane a long way from any houses.

Norman Hymers

[*Originally black powder was used in mines, hence the term powder house. Later this was replaced by dynamite produced by the ICI explosives division formed from the*

the old Dynamite Nobel Company. Many miners proudly bore black marks on their faces where coal particles had been driven into the skin by explosions. These marks were the sign of a true miner who had worked at the coal face.]

New Years Eve

I remember at midnight on New Years Eve all the colliery buzzers would sound to mark the beginning of the New Year. You could hear them one after another all round the district.

Vera Bradford

CHAPTER 4

Shops and public houses

Newgate Street, Bishop Auckland, *c.* 1920.

An advertisement for photographers, A&G Taylor of Newgate Street, proudly announces their Royal Appointment to Queen Victoria and the Royal Family.

Shops in Newgate Street

Newgate Street, Bishop Auckland has changed a lot in the past few years. The shops I can remember when I was a girl, and my mother and I went shopping, have all gone now.

Jones was a high class costumier and furrier. Their autumn window displays had leaves and berries. Doggarts Arcade held summer and winter sales, when you bought hats. Grays, known as 'Grays the sign of the clock' because it had a big clock hanging outside, sold clothing and materials. Watsons were ladies and gents outfitters. They cured fox skins, that people brought in, to be made into fox furs that were very fashionable at the time. They were worn, complete with the head and the tail, over the shoulder with a clip and a chain to hold them in place. I worked at Smiths, the cleaners, before I was married and the fox skins people brought in to us were sent over to Watsons.

Other shops were: Mudocks the drapers and Mrs Byers, who sold high class millinery. Snows were drapers, Raynors were drapers and outfitters and Wilkinsons were drapers and outfitters. Tim Brown was a gents hatter, T. Boughton, a high class gents outfitter. Both Sewells and Hedleys sold baby linen,

Nicholsons and Athertons were shoe shops. Taylors were photographers, as were Pickerings. Lowery offered photography and picture framing. Stamp sold china and jeweller. Hornsby was a jeweller. Todd the jeweller's shop was

This is Ivy, an antique Willow china doll, bought at J.J. Aubins Bazaar, Newgate Street, Bishop Auckland c. 1920.

followed by Westgarth, jeweller. Bradley purveyed fruit and vegetables. Hardesty was a fruiterer and florist. Lodge was another fruiterer. Maynards sold confectionery.

There was Holdens Bazaar and Aubins Bazaar, where reject china was displayed in clothes baskets round the shop. My china doll, Ivy, was bought at Aubins Bazaar in 1920. I made the clothes for her myself.

Cloughs sold hardware and china. Snaiths provided hardware, china and needlework. Julia Stephenson, needlework. Dunns were tailors. Alf Harburn was a chemist, as were Pickerings and Timothy Whites & Taylors. Messengers had a bakery and small tea room. Thirkell was a gents hairdresser. Herdmans sold pet foods and was a philatelist. Deftys were ironmongers and sold hardware and knitting wools. London & Newcastle Tea Stores were grocers and Maypole was another grocery store.

There was a cut price shop and on Thursdays during the war there was a queue, when the word went round that they had bananas. You took your ration book and if you bought something else you got some from under the counter. Lingfords were a high class grocers. I remember their autumn display. One window had a stuffed pheasant, heather and heather honey combs. The other window had special biscuits. My mother always made the biscuits we had at home, but I wanted some of those in

Manager Bill Taylor is pictured here with the staff of Duncan's grocery store, in 1941.

Lingfords window and she let me buy a quarter.

Burdess the pork butcher sold sandwiches at sixpence and pork dips for one penny. She had a big tray of dripping and dipped the roll in the hot fat to make the dips. The men leaving the football ground (Bishop Auckland) after the game used to queue for dips. They also sold 'penny ducks'. At Christmas their window display had a pigs head with an orange in its mouth and berry holly round the base of the window. Liptons were grocers, they had a jar of steeped peas in the window to show you how big their dried peas were after you had steeped them. The man used to pat the butter into shapes in the shop, when you bought it, with wooden butter pats.

Duff & Rowntrees were drapers and outfitters and then later became Gills furniture store. There was the Red Stamp Store, which is now Iceland frozen foods. Deans were family grocers. There was also Mrs Murdochs café. Smiths were dyers and cleaners, with the offices of Crawford, architect and the Refuge Insurance upstairs. Bishop Auckland Co-operative Society had a café, my mother used to buy flannel from the Co-op to make pit hoggers [working shorts] for my father to wear down the pit. Mrs Bells café was near the Kings Hall Arcade. It was very small, with only two or three tables. Mr Bell used to drive the United buses.

Vera Bradford

Newton Cap bridge with the Bridge Hotel on the far side of the river. The sign, which can be seen on the end wall, was painted by Varts, the decorators.

[*From this it can be seen that Bishop Auckland was a thriving town of small traders, supplying the mining communities around. Many of the shops stayed open late, particularly on a Saturday night when Newgate Street was a hive of activity.*]

Doggarts

I worked as a shoe buyer at Doggarts. They employed 350 full time and part time employees. It had its own transport, a garage behind the market place and a Works Department, opposite Wilson's Forge, with joiners and painters and decorators. When we had a fire drill everybody went over to the town hall. There was so many that they could not all get into the hall and many had to stand on the stairs to be checked by the department heads.

Frank Wilson

The Co-op

I also worked at the Co-op in Newgate Street, when it had horse-drawn bakery vans and a butchers department.

Frank Wilson

Newsagent

George Dowson had a newsagents shop, which was a wooden building at the bottom of Princes Street, opposite the Eden Theatre. He did a Sunday delivery service, by horse and flat cart, on Durham Road, Canney Hill, New Coundon and the Coundon area. My weekly buy was the Rainbow comic. George Dowson always wore an eye shield because he had suffered an injury in the First World War.

Vera Bradford

Grocer

I worked in the grocery trade for forty-five years, ending up at Presto in Bishop Auckland as manager. I started as an errand boy at seven shillings and sixpence a week, at Seaham Harbour, pushing a barrow delivering groceries. The barrow had a candle lantern on the shafts and I would often be delivering in the dark. We eventually got a bicycle with a carrier on the front. In the 1930s I used to go to ships to collect orders. We worked 52 hours a week, until 9 o'clock on a Saturday, with Wednesday off. When war was declared we only worked until 6 o'clock. I then got promoted to flour boy, packing half-stone bags of flour.

I came to Bishop to work for Duncans. We opened the first self-service shop in Bishop Auckland, in the old Kings Hall cinema, on Newgate Street.

Prices have changed a lot in the last few years. We had only four washing powders Persil, Oxydol, Acdo and Rinso. They were two pence for a small packet and three pence h'penny for a large packet. Bacon was seven pence and eight pence a pound. After the war, when we had bacon, when we opened up again after lunch the queue would be right down the street. We advertised that our butter came 'straight from ship to shop'.

Bill Taylor Snr

Reporter

When I left King James I Grammar School I got a job in the mens

The Sun Inn, Fore Bondgate. The inn now stands restored at the Beamish Museum.

department of Doggarts and was then taken on as a junior newspaper reporter. At that time four newspapers had offices in Bishop Auckland. *The Northern Echo, The Evening Gazette, The Evening Despatch* and *The Auckland Chronicle*. In those days we covered everything from council meetings, to court reporting, to theatrical productions and general news items.

Bill Taylor Jnr (Toronto, Canada)

A Plethora of Pubs

I came across this list of the pubs that used to be in Bishop Auckland in the 1890s.

Above: Regulars of the Bridge Hotel, Newton Cap in Bishop Auckland, are seen here with landlord Mark Stephenson (in shirtsleeves) in the 1920s. The little boy is George Stephenson.

Above Right: Ball players at the Sportsman Inn, Canney Hill at the turn of the century. The shiny black boots and the immaculate turn out show how seriously the game was taken. Note the size of the ball for such a fast, highly competitive game.

Alma, South Church Road; Angel, Market Place; Bay Horse, Woodhouses; Bay Horse, Bondgate; Black Boy, Newgate Street; Black Horse, Newton Cap; Bridge Hotel, Newton Cap; Commercial, Market Place; Court Inn, High Bondgate; Crown, North Bondgate; Derby, Tenters Street; Durham Hotel, South Road; Edinburgh Castle, Bondgate; Fleece Hotel, Bondgate; George Hotel, Bondgate; Green Tree, Cockton Hill Road; Kings Arms, Market Place; Masons Arms, Etherley Moor; Mitre, South Road; Newton Cap, Newton Cap; Post Office, Newgate Street; Pollards, Etherley Lane; Queens Head, Market Place; Red Lion, Newgate Street; Seven Stars, High Bondgate; Shepherds Inn, Bondgate; Spirit Vaults, Fore Bondgate; Sportsman, Market Place; Station Hotel, South Road; Sun Inn, Bondgate; Talbot Hotel, Market Place; Theatre Bar, Newgate Street; Three Blue Bells, Newgate Street; Three Tuns, Newgate Street; Three Tuns, Bondgate; Tile Sheds, South Road; Turf Hotel, Newgate Street; Victoria, West Road; Volunteer Arms, Newgate Street; Waterloo, Newgate Street; Wear Valley

Hotel, Newgate Street; Wear Hotel, Wear Chare; Wheatsheaf, Bondgate; White Lion, Newgate Street; Welcome, Waldron Street.

Beer Houses
Cumberland Inn, South Road; Gaunless Inn, Durham Chare; Harp Inn, Thompson Street; Latherbrush, Etherley Lane; Maid of Erin, West Road; Miners Arms, Teneters Street; Nags Head, South Church Lane; Vulcan Hotel, Peel Street.

Bill Taylor Jnr (Toronto, Canada)

[Later the Volunteer Arms became Wrights Hotel. The Gaunless was known locally as The Jigger. There was a difference between hotels and inns, which were allowed to sell all drinks as well as providing food and accommodation, and beer houses, which were licensed to sell only beers and porter. It is interesting that for such a small town there were so many places where drinks could be bought. This is an indication of the large influx of miners, coke workers, railwaymen and navvies which took place from 1810. Of particular interest is the fact that there were twelve pubs in the two Bondgates and fifteen between the railway station and the market place, with others within a few hundred yards of the main street.]

The Bridge Hotel

My grandfather, Mark Stephenson, was the landlord of the Bridge Hotel, at Newton Cap, in the 1920s. He died in 1928 and my grandmother, Jane Stephenson, continued as landlady until the pub closed in the early 1950s. She was the landlady for thirty-three years. My grandmother died in 1959. The previous landlord, before my grandparents, was James Shield who was a family friend for many years.

Sybil Gibson

Ball Alley

The Sportsman Inn, Canney Hill, had a ball alley where the local men played handball against the gable end of the pub. It was later turned into a car park and is now a restaurant. The miners from Auckland Park colliery played handball there.

Vera Bradford

CHAPTER 5

Workhouse and hospital

These stark red buildings housed the Childrens Home in Escombe Road, Bishop Auckland.

This property is what remains of the old workhouse buildings. The premises are now used for offices by the Bishop Auckland General Hospital.

Workhouse

I commenced service with the Local Authority in August 1925. I was born on the 16th November 1903 in Wood Street, Bishop Auckland. My father was a miner working at Leasingthorne Colliery. We moved from Bishop Auckland to Coundon so that he could be near his work. I was good at art and applied to the Bishop Auckland Rural Council, whose offices were in Craddock Street. The surveyor was Mr Charles Heslop. I was lucky enough to be employed by him, on a temporary basis, as an assistant surveyor.

The terms of employment were that I would work for three years without pay. My father found it difficult to keep me without pay, so I applied to the land agent of Bolcow Vaughan & Company.

I stayed there until 1926 when I was successful in obtaining a position as shorthand typist with the Urban District Council of Bishop Auckland, the Auckland Board of Guardians, the Hospital Board and the Registrar of Births and Deaths. The offices were in No. 56 North Bondgate. The Medical Officer of Health, in Craddock Street, was Dr Penfold.

Many patients were admitted to Bishop Auckland hospital, which was a Poor Law hospital and only occupied by people on relief. Maternity cases were dealt with at Princes Street Maternity Home, which belonged to Durham County Council and was a private nursing home - people who went there had to pay. Other people went to St Monicas Home.

The casual wards were in the building

The original wooden buildings of the general hospital, as they are seen today.

that is now used as the supplies department in the hospital, the old buildings having been demolished. Each patient being admitted was bathed, deloused, given a meal and put to bed. Their clothes were cleaned and made ready for departure. They were occupied for a full day in the gardens. All the vegetables were grown by the Poor Law and also the bread was cooked on the premises, by a man called Robson - an old inmate of the workhouse. All admissions to the workhouse had to go past the gatekeeper, whose name was Chapman. The labour master and the matron were Mr and Mrs Thompson.

The atmosphere in the hospital was one of despair. Poor people had nowhere else to go and were housed in the workhouse and seemed to be glad they had somewhere to sleep. Casual wards in the region were all on the notice board in the casual ward.

Inmates admitted one day were kept the following day to work for their keep and discharged the day after that. Most of them seemed to be well shod, if not they were dealt with by Mr Denham, the cobbler, who repaired their boots or shoes so they were all right before they left the building.

Mr Sands

Relief

In 1921 the miners had a strike and all the collieries were closed. Soup kitchens were organised and people who were unable to manage were given relief on loan. I was earning twelve shillings a week, which was considered sufficient without recourse to the Poor Law. Of course during that time nobody paid any rates or rent, all the money that went into the home was needed to keep body and soul together, so mainly it was spent on food.

The Relieving Officer for Bishop Auckland was Mr Joe Holliday and he was responsible for issuing vouchers for relief. Relief was only minimal. On one occasion a family was so numerous that the committee decided to tell the Relieving Officer that he must have a word with the applicant. He told him that he had to curtail his deliberations and behave himself, because they were not able to give him any more relief. Unable to obtain an assurance that the couple could control themselves, he was obliged to inform them that any more children would have to be kept using the present money as no extra could be allowed.

Mr Sands

Workhouse Master

Mr Robson, the master of the workhouse, was a very keen temperance man and would not allow alcohol on the premises. He spent a lot of time dealing with the work of the Temperance Movement.

Mr Sands

Suppliers

Contracts were tendered every year for the supply of goods to the workhouse. The food was supplied by a Newcastle firm and the meat by Manners [butchers of Bishop Auckland, who are still in existence]. Any bits of material that were brought as a sample were passed on to the sewing room, so that they could be made into handkerchiefs, floor cloths or dusters. Nothing was ever wasted.

Mr Sands

A Days Work

There was a large workhouse I remember. Especially vivid is the memory of huge numbers of homeless people steaming out of the hospital laundry, where they worked for a days keep.

Margery Graham

Board of Guardians

The members of the old Board of Guardians of the workhouse, in 1925, were Mr J.C.B. Hendy, chairman, Mr James Burns of Coundon, Mr Frank Blenkinsop of Leaholme, Mr Johnny Greenwood, Bishop Auckland, Alderman Bob Middlewood and Revd Hodgson.

Mr Sands

Housekeepers

You could go to the workhouse and get a woman out to come and work, do your housekeeping and that. On the front street on Bowman Terrace there was a Mr McLean in the second house, he'd lost his wife. He had a son called 'Bandy' McLean because he played in a band. That Mr McLean got a woman out of the workhouse, she was there a year or two, and eventually he married her.

Vera Bradford

Wayfarers

I remember the poor people who had left the workhouse and were walking to the next one at Durham, because they could only stay one night in each workhouse. As they passed through Coundon Gate they would knock on your door and ask for a glass of water or anything else you would give them.

Vera Bradford

Waifs and Strays

The Children's Home was in the stark red buildings on Escomb Road, behind the hospital. One building was for the boys and one for the girls. There was a field at the back where the children could play with a few swings. They were made to go out and play in all weathers, they were very poorly dressed and must have been frozen. It was a very hard regime. Some of the children were orphans and some were just unwanted and ended up in the home.

Marion Blackett

A Pauper's Grave

The paupers who died were buried in unmarked graves along the River Gaunless, at the bottom of the cemetery. From Durham Chare you walked along the riverside and there were two cottages, there was an apple tree outside.

Vera Bradford

Hospitals and Nursing

Before the National Health Service, Bishop Auckland hospital was simply a collection of huts - serious cases went to Darlington or Newcastle to be treated. I was a young nurse at the time and the chronic wards for old people were basic to say the least. One of the sisters on the old men's ward was eccentric to say the least. Every Friday we young nurses would have to start at one end of the ward giving each old man an enema, whether or not it was wanted or needed by the old dears. One young male nurse got so fed up with the whole palaver that he locked himself in the linen cupboard one Christmas day and proceeded to drink a whole bottle of gin. Three porters had to knock the door down and put the happy but paralytic young man to bed.

Marjorie Graham

Kriegsgefangene

There were German POWs billeted in the hospital, mostly young boys. The way these soldiers decorated the wards at Christmas was fantastic, they made an especially good job of the children's wards.

Marjorie Graham

Enemy in Sight

There was a wall along Escomb Road, with barbed wire along the top, in front of the huts, which are still there. These huts were built for prisoners of war needing hospital treatment. I believe they had heated coke stoves. We used to walk along from Etherley Lane school to Escomb Road, where we lived. When we got to Latherbrush bridge we sometimes met a crocodile of German prisoners of war being taken to the recreation ground, from the hospital, to play football. They were made to wait until we crossed the bridge. We used to run across the bridge because they were Germans but looking back on it they were just very young boys who no doubt only wanted to go home.

Marion Blackett

Isolation Hospital

My eldest brother contacted scarlet fever when he was twelve and was confined in the fever hospital at Tindall Crescent for about six weeks. His bedroom had to be sealed up after being fumigated for weeks.

Marjorie Graham

Not a Mystery Tour

The staff at the hospital had a mystery tour once a year, but it was never a mystery because the bus always went to Reeth!

Marjorie Graham

Staff

At the beginning of the health service, in early 1949, the matron at Bishop Auckland hospital was Miss Dinning. The deputy matron was Miss Watson and the night superintendent was Miss Stella Bainbridge, whose father was known as Honest John Bainbridge.

Mr Sands

A Military Hospital

Quite a lot of work had been done by military personnel during the war years and records had been kept of all military personnel who had been dealt with at the hospital. The number of beds available during the war was 625, most of them housed in huts that had been built specially for this purpose. On each ward were 48 beds and it was very crowded. After the war the number of beds in each ward was reduced to 24.

Mr Sands

Entertainment

In the early days of the health service a social club was formed. The money made from the various garden parties was eventually used to buy equipment for entertainment purposes. We also obtained a gramophone, record player, loudspeaker and we were also very lucky in obtaining tennis equipment for the tennis courts. We could hold regular tennis tournaments for the benefit of patients. We obtained a projector and film shows were organised through the various organisations such as MGM, Warner Brothers and Columbia. Regular film shows were given to the patients of the General Hospital, the Lady Eden, Tindale Crescent and Homelands.

Mr Sands

League of Friends

Every year the League of Friends organised a function, with stalls and a well known speaker. We got Newton Aycliffe Pipe Band to play in the street and the hospital staff used to go out and collect money. Very good support was given to this particular function. The money raised was spent on the patients and the hospital. In one instance Homelands hospital wanted a lot of money spent on the day ward and this money was provided by the League of Friends. They also provided extras at Christmas time, for the patients.

Mr Sands

Convalescence

We had two hospitals, which were used as convalescent homes - one was Horn Hall at Stanhope and the other was Leazes hospital at Wolsingham. Stanhope dealt with male patients and Leazes with female patients. I was also able to arrange for convalescence in Cumberland and also for children, at Scarborough.

Mr Sands

[Mr Sands, who worked for both the workhouse and the hospital, recorded his memories before his death. His daughter made the tape available for his memories to be used in this book.]

School Medical Care

Routine medical checks were carried out at school and children were given free milk if necessary. I loved the break at school when we were given a bottle of milk and a digestive biscuit. There was a school dentist and of course 'nitty Nora'. We all dreaded the nitty nurse in case she actually found any nits in our hair, which would have been mortifying, we would have died of shame.

Marjorie Graham

District Nurse

The district nurse was a dedicated soul who got around on a bicycle in all weathers. Her name was Miss Pallister and she was well respected in the area. Most women had their babies at home then, often helped by a neighbour or amateur midwife. Some of the helpers were very good, although it had to be said that many were more of a hindrance.

Marjorie Graham

CHAPTER 6

Wartime

Colonel Armstrong proudly leads the 2nd Volunteer Battalion D.L.I. They had returned from service in South Africa in the Boer War. We see them marching down Newgate Street, Bishop Auckland, passing the end of Tenters Street, on their way to a reception at the town hall. The crowds thickened to such an extent further down the street that the Adjutant, D'Arcy Hilyard, had his foot trodden on and had to be helped out of the parade. That night the Volunteers were entertained to a banquet in the town hall. The following night they were invited to attend a performance of *The Rajah of Ranjapore*, at the Eden Theatre, as guests of the manager Robert Addison. The 2nd D.V.L.I., based in Bishop Auckland, was one of the few Volunteer battalions to serve in South Africa during the Boer War.

Soldiers sent this embroidered card home from the Front in the First World War.

A Soldier of the Queen

My great grandfather, Jigger Morland, walked from Bishop Auckland to Richmond, in Yorkshire, in 1891 and joined the Yorkshire Regiment. It was discovered, though, that he had a valvular disorder of the heart and he was discharged. He then managed to join the 6th Battalion Durham Light Infantry, based in Bishop Auckland and went with them to the Boer War. He did not mention his heart problem. When he was discharged, after the regiment returned from South Africa, having served his time, his medals were sent to him by post. In 1908, when the territorials were started, he was one of the first to join. In 1914 the 6th Battalion Territorials, of which he was a member, was sent to the Western front in France and he was wounded twice. His nineteen year old son, James, who

had also joined the 6th Battalion, served with his father until he was killed by a sniper. His father carried his body back to the casualty clearing station behind the lines. His other son, Gunner Joseph Morland RA, who saw service in China, Singapore and Hong Kong, having joined in 1933, was killed at Malta while returning home in 1940. When Jigger died, in 1953, he was the last survivor, in Bishop Auckland, of the Boer War. In his later years he became somewhat eccentric and finally put himself into the workhouse, where he died.

Gavin Bake

Off to the Front

I can remember the DLI going off to the First World War. We lived in Surtees Street and we sat on the wall in Lower Waldron Street watching the

Private John Richardson (1891–1916).

the train go by, with all the soldiers waving to us.

Amy Hodgson

Death of an Artist

Private John Richardson, of the 22nd Durham Light Infantry, Pioneer Battalion, was born in 1891 at Hunwick. He was married only one day before he went back to the front and was wounded by 'blue on blue' fire [friendly fire, from British guns] on 23 October 1916. He died at Roen and is buried in the cemetery at St Severs. John was a very talented amateur artist and had a studio above Bellerby's old shop in South Road, Bishop Auckland, where he gave tuition to local people interested in art. His work was exhibited in Bishop Auckland town hall in 1913.

Amy Hodgson

Letters Home

John Richardson's nephew, John Parkin, wanted to know how his uncles sent letters home from France and was told a huge bird flew with them in his beak. When he asked if he could see it his uncle sent him a sketch on one of his letters.

Amy Hodgson

John Richardson with his wife, Jennie, the day after their marriage.

John Richardson drew this and sent it to his nephew from France. It shows a large bird bringing the letters home.

Zeppelin Raid

A German zeppelin dropped twelve bombs on Gurney Valley in the First World War. One hit a house in Close House and a little boy was killed. The Mine Rescue Team from Black Boy Pit dug them out. One bomb nearly hit Eldon Lane Club. The zeppelin was trying to hit Black Boy Pit. The bombs fell after some people had gone to bed and some of the women gathered up their children and ran to their mother's houses. They just gathered up their clothes and ran but unfortunately someone dropped certain items of underclothing. The next morning as the miners went on shift they found the garments and soon the story went round the village that the zeppelin was flown by women.

Close House Womens Institute

John's Richardson's mother and sister.

Bomb Crater

I remember the bombs dropped in the First World War. They came with a zeppelin and they dropped one in Coronation school yard. I can remember being taken to be shown the hole. I can only remember the noise, we thought it was a thunderstorm.

Amy Hodgson

A Very Brave Man

When the zeppelin dropped the bomb in Coronation school yard, during the First World War, my grandfather Richard Walton dug it out.

The bomb didn't explode and being a man who loved children he was concerned about the children at the school. He had an allotment opposite the school and went to his shed and got a spade and dug out the bomb. My aunt remembers the nose cone of the bomb being kept in a cupboard at home, until the school were wanting to set up a museum and it was given to the school. I remember it being in a cupboard in the second hall when I was a pupil there. My grandfather was a very unassuming man and worked at Fishburn colliery in charge of the tradesmen.

Don Wylie

79

This row of houses was hit by a bomb in Close House during the zeppelin attack on Black Boy Pit, in which a small boy was killed. His body was recovered by the Black Boy Mine Rescue Team.

Coronation school and playground. This is where a bomb, dropped by a zeppelin in the First World War, landed.

Peace

At the end of the First World War, I was at Warton Street Church of England school at Coundon. I was about six. We walked in procession to Leaholme Lane Ends, near Hartley House. We were given a bag with a bun in it and a medal on a ribbon.

Vera Bradford

Armistice

I can remember the end of the war. There was a teacher, Miss Harburn, she was a student teacher and we called her Miss Agnes. They didn't have telephones at the school then or nothing. She was sent down to the market place to hear what was going on and bring messages back. I can remember there was a thin layer of snow on the ground. That was on 11 November 1918. After the war there was this big stand put up in the market place and we went from the school. I wasn't very big you know and I stood behind this chair and I can remember reading it. I've never forgotten it, Sir Henry Havelock-Alan. That was what was written on the back of the chair.

Amy Hodgson

Follow the Guns

I joined the 70th West Riding Field Regiment of Territorials in Bradford before the Second World War. After being called up we were sent to France to fight a rearguard action, just before Dunkirk. We arrived on the last day of the Dunkirk evacuation and were recalled having never fired a shot. We sailed out of Cherbourg. We were sent to guard the aerodrome at Drem, outside Edinburgh. We had an observation post on the top of Berwick Law, overlooking the Firth of Forth. We were destined for Norway but the evacuation at Narvick had started and we were stopped. I was posted to the 1st Medium Regiment RA. They had come out at Dunkirk and had left all their guns on the beaches. They had been sent to Uppingham in Leicestershire, but when we arrived there they had moved on and nobody could tell us where they were. We reported to the local police station and the desk sergeant, after a great number of telephone calls, said 'The war is over for you lads. You are going to New Zealand to a place called West Auckland. Report to the RTO at Leicester.' We were then sent to the RTO at Doncaster, who put us on a train to West Auckland in County Durham, where the regimental headquarters was based in Brewery House, which is now the Manor House Hotel. We caught up with the guns on the beach at Seaham. 1/3 Battery headquarters was then moved to Witton le Wear and we became a training regiment for new recruits. The green at West Auckland was the parade square and many a recruit broke in his new army boots there. We left West Auckland on the 26 May 1942, for overseas service. While in Witton le Wear, I met a local farmer's daughter, Emily Findlay, and we married. After the war we settled in the area and I bought a garage business in Howden le Wear.

Douglas Wilkes

Brewery House, West Auckland is where the Medium Artillery had their headquarters during the early part of the Second World War. The building is now the Manor House Hotel.

Commanding Officer

The commanding officer of the 1st Medium Regiment, when it was based at Brewery House, was Lt Colonel Robert Grant MC. He moved when the headquarters was moved to Witton le Wear. The officer's mess was in Witton Castle - the home of Sir William Chater. Mrs Grant joined her husband there.

Douglas Wilkes

A Cushy Billet

The commanding officer of the artillery, based in part of Brewery House, used to mess with us. We lived in part of the building, another part was the brewery offices and the army had a part at the front. The officers used to have their dinner in our part of the house.

Peter Monk

Observer Corps

My father, Sydney Monk, was the commanding officer at the Observer Corps, in West Auckland, during the Second World War. They had a post on the top of West Auckland colliery pit heap. I remember we used to climb up there. They had a wooden hut on the top of the pit heap.

Peter Monk

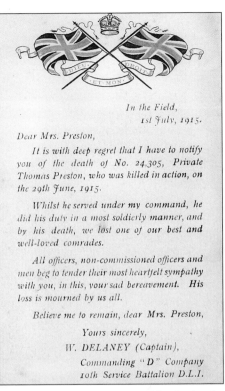

In the Field,
1st July, 1915.

Dear Mrs. Preston,

It is with deep regret that I have to notify you of the death of No. 24,305, Private Thomas Preston, who was killed in action, on the 29th June, 1915.

Whilst he served under my command, he did his duty in a most soldierly manner, and by his death, we lost one of our best and well-loved comrades.

All officers, non-commissioned officers and men beg to tender their most heartfelt sympathy with you, in this, your sad bereavement. His loss is mourned by us all.

Believe me to remain, dear Mrs. Preston,

Yours sincerely,

W. DELANEY (Captain),

Commanding "D" Company
10th Service Battalion D.L.I.

WHICH WILL HE HOIST FIRST.

Pte T.B. Cook
4TH Sherwood's
Etherley
V.A. Hospital
6/8/1917

Above: This notice was received by the families of servicemen who were killed in the First World War. Above Right: An excerpt from the autograph book kept by Cicely Lumley, who was a nurse at the Etherley Military Hospital during the First World War. Soldiers from many regiments signed the book and in many cases entered drawings and poems. Cicely must have been a very popular nurse according to the inscriptions. The staff at the Etherley hospital did sterling work, looking after many injured servicemen between 1914 and 1918.

D-day Build Up

I remember my father telling me that, just before D-day, they used to park lots of military vehicles overnight, up the lane by the side of West Auckland Brewery. They came down from Scotland on their way to the south coast and parked. I suppose they didn't want them to be seen, moving with their lights, at night. Many of them were loaded with ammunition, which looking back on it could have been nasty if there had been an air raid.

Peter Monk

A Dodgy Situation

When we were based at West Auckland, in 1941, there was an air raid and bombs were dropped behind the village, near Etherley. We had live ammunition stored in a wood behind the village. After the raid we went up there to see if it had been hit, but fortunately it had escaped.

Douglas Wilkes

Daylight Raid

They dropped a load of bombs one September afternoon, near Toft Hill and near Greenfields. My sister worked for the Drummonds, who lived in a big white house behind St Helens. She was resting on the sofa when the bombs dropped and went out to look. She found the nose cone of one of them and I had it for years. I had a big collection of shrapnel, but it was all buried under our house when it was built.

Sonny Dowthwaite

Not Safe

When we lived at Etherley, during the Second World War, there were five bombs dropped in Tom's field. I think they were just dropping them anywhere to get rid of them, they were just small holes. A little boy was killed, he was an evacuee from Hebburn. He was buying sweets and the shop keeper told him to get off home. He was killed by shrapnel.

Amy Hodgson

Tank Traps

There were concrete road blocks in Durham Road, as you came out of the market place, to stop tanks if there was an invasion. The space between them was just wide enough to allow one car to go through.

Vera Bradford

A Wartime Childhood

In 1941 we lived in a white cottage that stood where Chamberlain Phipps factory is now, on the lane going up to Woodhouses. It had a big farm gate with a high wall at the front and a low wall at the back. We used to sit on the front wall and watch the tanks go by. The soldiers used to train up the lane. I went to Cockton Hill school and walked there. When you got to Cabin Gate we used to have to walk through big concrete blocks set in the road. On each corner, opposite Elliots garage, there were soldiers in concrete machine gun posts, with machine guns. The soldiers were billeted in St Helens Old Hall.

Joyce Jennings

Manoeuvres

My grandmother, Jane Stephenson, ran the Bridge Hotel near Newton Cap bridge. There was a pill box on the other side of the bridge. Once, during the war, the pub was commandeered by the army to carry out manoeuvres. Soldiers in the upstairs windows were defending the bridge. They must have used live ammunition, because after the exercise was over some children found a hand grenade down on the Batts, it exploded and one little boy was killed.

Sybil Gibson

The Injin House

There was a building at the bottom of Newton Cap, with a big chimney and double doors. In the 1930s it was the town's incinerator and was run by a man called Mr Robb. He didn't like children and used to chase us away. He retired and a man called Harry Robb took over, no relation. I got on with him and during the war he used to let me help with baling the waste paper collection that was stored there. He showed me how to use the hand baler and tie the special knots that were used. You put a piece of cardboard in the bottom and then the paper on the top, then another piece of cardboard and pulled a lever and it was compressed. Then it was tied with string, given a number with BAUDC [Bishop Aukland Urban District Council] on a label, weighed, entered in a book and stacked waiting for the lorries to collect. The waste was put into the boiler and I can still remember the roar up the chimney as it was burnt. Sometimes the stacks were like a big staircase which went up to the roof and you could climb up there and touch the girders. I never understood why it was always called the Injin House, because there was only a big boiler in there. I asked my father and he told me that it was where the big pumps used to be, to pump the water up to the town before they built the Water Works at West Mills.

Sybil Gibson

Fire Watching

We had a place over Chipchase and Woods' office, next to the Gentleman's Club in Victoria Avenue, Bishop Auckland, with camp beds. We had two nights on and one off

Jack Vart during his days in the D.L.I.

and were there from 11p.m. to 8a.m. There was the Brownless brothers, Sid and Jack, Nellie Dowson - who was the manageress of Maynards the sweet shop, Orson Chapman - who worked at Hepworths the tailors and Winnie Grey - who worked in a shop. She was the relief if anybody was off. We were never called out, but we had our training on incendiary bombs in the old station goods yard. The council organised it all. If you were at the pictures when the alarm went they would flash your name on the screen and you had to report for duty. I never had a tin hat.

One chap called Robinson used to bring a dust pan and shovel with him and used to cook a pigeon on the fire for his supper, there was always a big fire in

West Mills Water Works, in their heyday. This attractive local beauty spot has long since gone. Its gardens were particularly noteworthy. Some of the trees can still be seen, standing in front of the rugby ground.

the room. The smell was terrible and he used to offer us some. He always said 'its cooked to a turn', but nobody wanted any.

Bill Taylor Snr

Gas Masks

We all had gas masks. I had mine in a leather case, but Bill kept his in a cardboard box. The children were only young and Valerie had a Mickey Mouse gas mask. We had a baby one for young Bill but he was never inside it. We never tried because we thought he would scream the place down. After the war, the council knocked on the door and took the baby one away, but they put up a big notice in the town hall and we had to take the others back.

Gladys Taylor

Rationing

I came to Bishop Auckland, in 1941, as manager of Duncans the grocers, at 27 Newgate Street. You registered for rations with a shop and we marked your book when you had your rations, or we cut the coupons out. Some people registered with two or three shops in the hope of getting extras, like bananas, when they came in because you tended to give those to your registered customers. We had to take the coupons to the food office, which is now Greaves & Ramsey, next to the Wear Valley Hotel. I tried to make certain that nobody got more that their share, although a letter came from Anthony Eden [later Prime Minister], signed Sir Anthony Eden, Bart complaining that the rations for Windlestone Hall were not enough. People always called me Mr Duncan and one old lady I met after the war, said I was 'the finest gentleman in the town, always fair with the rations.' I remembered her, she was one of the ladies who used to come into the shop wearing black shawls over their heads. You got 3 ounces of bacon, 3 ounces of fat - either butter, lard or margarine, a quarter of tea a month and 8 ounces of sugar [aside from tea, rations were weekly]. Tinned goods were on points, which you cut out. A tin of milk was 2 points. You could get dried egg, which wasn't rationed, and dried milk but nobody liked the dried milk much.

Bill Taylor Snr

Reserved Occupation

I worked for Duncans during the war and I wanted to join the Wrens, but as I was in the food trade they wouldn't let me go. So I gave my notice in, but I got a letter from the Government telling me I had to go back. I stayed there until the children came along.

Gladys Taylor

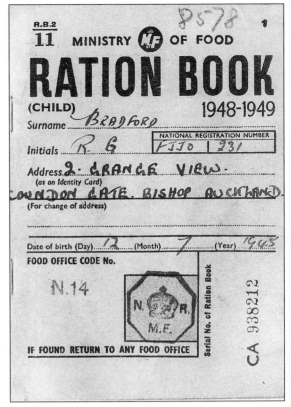

Rationing of food and clothes continued after the war. Ration books like this were issued to all adults and special ones were issued for children.

Air Raid Precautions

We had strips of brown sticky paper criss-crossed over the shop window. When the air raid warning sounded, during the day, we had heavy steel shutters that went over the window. These were kept in the cellar and we had to carry them up. It took ages to fit them, in fact the all clear could sound before we got them up, then we had to take them down again.

Bill Taylor Snr

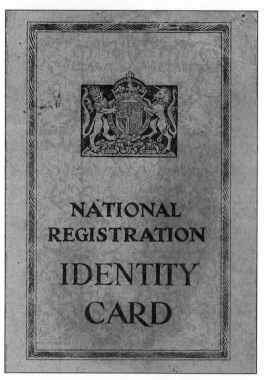

Above: During the Second World War all civilians were issued with a National Identity Card, which was supposed to be shown on request. The majority of ordinary people rarely had to show their cards. Above Right: The order of the service for the unveiling of the Newfield War Memorial, in 1922.

Essential Warwork

During the Second World War I worked at Smiths, the cleaners. A lot of the work we did was for the officers stationed at Spennymoor. We could only take so much civilian work, so on a Monday morning they had to queue outside the shop hoping to get one of the tickets which were allowed for non-army people. They used to come from all over - Kelloe, West Cornforth and Ferryhill and suchlike. We also had an allocation of only two household goods, such as curtains and bedspreads each week. There was a fashion for dying white marcela bedspreads blue or pink, but you had to wait your turn. We also cleaned

kid gloves, but I never thought that worked so well.

In the shop we had a selection of ladies hats and we dyed and remodelled felt or velour ladies hats. The ladies would come in and try on those on show and chose how they wanted theirs to look. We always said they looked nice, even if they didn't. We had an express service of two days. This was used a lot by cricketers, who wanted their flannels cleaned for the next weekend. The clothes to be cleaned used to be put in large wickerwork baskets with leather straps. They were sent to Bishop Auckland railway station to be sent to Dewsbury. One year there was heavy snow and the train could not get beyond Ferryhill with the cleaned

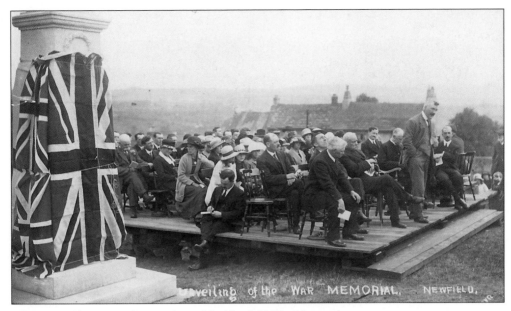

The guests of honour at the unveiling of the Newfield War Memorial.

clothes. One of the officer's batmen came for his officers cleaning but it had not come back. He said his officer would be very angry and that he would get into trouble, so we gave him the ticket and let him go to Ferryhill and get his stuff out of the skip. I was called to go for interview to be sent on war work but my boss gave me a letter to take saying, that as we did a lot of military cleaning, I was already on war work. I went for the interview at Spennymoor but was not called up.

Vera Bradford

Munitions

I went to the Immaculate Conception School in Darlington, then I came to Bishop Auckland. When war came, in 1939, I got a job at what became the munitions factory, at Aycliffe, in the wages department. There was only twelve of us to start with and only green fields and a farm. At the end there was 30,000 people working there and we did the wages. I remember Winston Churchill coming and one of the girls in our office presented him with a cigar. The wages had to be done on punch cards, which had to be fed into a machine. I think this was the beginning of computers.

Katherine MacGannon.

CHAPTER 7

Pastimes and holidays

A replica of the Sir Thomas Lipton trophy.

The Eden Arms Hotel, in West Auckland was used as the headquarters of West Auckland Football Club. This is where the Thomas Lipton trophy was held until it was moved to the Working Men's Club.

World Beaters

People of Durham county are really proud to remember that it was West Auckland Football Club who represented Great Britain in the very first 'world cup' competition, during Easter 1909, and won it. The competition was held in Turin, Italy with teams from the host country, Germany, Switzerland and Great Britain taking part. The trophy was presented to the winners by Sir Thomas Lipton. He was a millionaire with business interests in Britain and Italy. To start with the English Football Association were asked to nominate a team, but they decided not to. Sir Thomas wanted Great Britain to be represented, but how West Auckland ended up as the team isn't really known. The story goes that an

employee of Sir Thomas happened to be a referee in the northern league and it's likely that he picked a substitute team from that league - West Auckland Town. The team was mostly made up of coal miners and so they struggled to raise the money to make the trip to Italy. Some even pawned their possessions in order to do so.

Their determination paid off, as they beat Stuttgart of Germany 2-0, on the way to beating FC Winterhour of Switzerland 2-0 in the final, in Turin stadium on 12 April 1909. So, the first world cup had been won by a team of relatively unknown amateurs, who had to finance the excursion themselves. They were not out of pocket because they did make some money from the trip. In 1911 the competition was held in Italy again. As reigning champions,

West Auckland was invited back to defend the trophy. They beat Red Star of Switzerland 2-0 on the way to the final, where they beat Juventus of Italy 6-1 on 17 April 1911. Sir Thomas had said that the team winning the trophy on two consecutive tournaments would keep it.

This time though, the celebrations on returning home were short lived. Because of the financial problems the tour had caused, the club had to find £40 quickly. As their only asset was the trophy, an arrangement was made with Mrs Lancaster, the landlady of the Wheatsheaf Hotel, which was used as the club's headquarters. The agreement involved a loan of £40 by Mrs Lancaster to the club with the trophy as security, which she would keep until the money was returned. She kept it for fifty years! In 1960, club officials tracked down Mrs Lancaster – she was still alive and living in Liverpool. She obviously still had all her faculties, as she drove a hard bargain before handing over the trophy in return for £100.

On its return, the trophy was put on display in the Eden Arms in West Auckland, which was the home of the club secretary, Mr Syd Dowthwaite. It stayed on show and it was only when the Jules Rimmet trophy was stolen, in 1966, that Mr Dowthwaite began to lock it away. In January 1994 the trophy, which was then in West Auckland Working Mens Club, was stolen. Despite the best efforts of the police, and the offer of a big reward, the trophy hasn't been found. Luckily it was insured by Cornhill insurance and so a replica has been made. To this end Mr John Harrison of Finlays Jewellers, Bishop Auckland was contacted. He knew a Sheffield silversmith, Mr Jack Spenser, who has

now produced a replica, working from photographs and videos. The replica was sponsored by Van den Berg Foods, and will again be kept in the Working Mens Club, in a specially constructed cabinet sponsored by Mr Bill Moody of Rushlift Limited. It is with great pride, and thanks to the sponsors of the West Auckland Football Club, that the club again has the Sir Thomas Lipton trophy. We are still involved with Liptons, they sponsor games for us, but Liptons is all export now. Their top sales manager comes to see us every month or so and watches games. When the world cup was played over here in 1966, our cup was down at the Eden Arms. The Italians played at Middlesbrough and they all came to see it and they wanted to take it back with them. That was the Italian national team, but a lot of the players were from Juventus.

Stuart Alderson, General Manager of West Auckland FC

Picnics

Picnics at Dam Head and Bedburn Woods were lovely. Bedburn being particularly special because it was a riot of bluebells, violets and primroses and there was a lovely steam running through to complete the idyllic scene.

Vera Bradford

FA Amateur Cup

I used to follow Bishop Auckland football club when I was about 14. I always went to the Kingsway end behind the goal. I had sixpence, it cost

The Ladies Matting Club at Fylands, *c.* 1910.

Above: Eleanor Wood of Fylands watches German gypsies go by, with her son William and daughter 'Tissy', at the turn of the century.

Above Right: Eleanor Wood poses, in her finery, for a classical picture of the period.

Bishop Auckland Amateur Football Club won the FA Amateur Cup in 1938, after extra time. The match against Willington was played at Roker Park, in Sunderland. The Auckland team won 3-0. A hat trick was scored by Wensley (middle row, second on the left). This was the seventh time Bishop Auckland had won the cup, they went on to win a record ten times and were the only club to win it in consecutive seasons - 1954/55, 1955/56 and 1956/57. The club was founded, in 1886, by the theological students of Oxford and Cambridge, who studied with the Bishop of Durham at Auckland Castle. This is why the club is known as The Two Blues.

two pence to get in and I bought two penny worth of Pomfret cakes every Saturday. I remember watching the old grandstand collapsing with the heavy snow. I was at King James school and we were outside and suddenly the grandstand, which we could see from the school, just gave way. Then they built a new one. When Bishop played Willington in the 1938/39 final at Sunderland, I went to the match. Afterwards I went to the Sunderland Empire to see Fats Waller.

Donald Callender

[*This was a record, seventh win of the FA Amatuer Cup for Bishop Auckland. The final score was 3-0, after extra time. Wensley scored a hat trick during extra time.*]

Easter

Easter Sundays were a highlight. Families from Leasingthorne, Coundon and Leaholme used to walk to the Bishops Park where games and competitions were held and the children bowled their Easter eggs down the slopes. Whitsuntide and August Bank holidays were the same, with Punch and Judy shows.

Vera Bradford

Lantern Shows

The Temperance Hall in Bishop Auckland put on lantern shows on Sunday nights, which cost a penny to get in. My father used to walk to Bishop to see them.

Vera Bradford

Sunday School

The first Sunday school I attended was part of the Methodists. I remember the teachers with affection and I particularly enjoyed the Sunday school trips to Redcar. We would get sixpence and our mothers would pack us some sandwiches and off we would go on the OK bus, singing our heads off.

Vera Bradford

Itchy Baize

Itchy baize was a game played by marking out numbered squares on the ground. You threw your itchy dabber into the squares and had to hop, making certain you did not stand on the lines. I believe it is also known as hopscotch but we called it itchy baize.

Vera Bradford

Pole Bays

We played pole bays, which was similar to pole vaulting. You had a big pole and saw who could jump the furthest. We also played itchy dabbers.

Mary Simpson

A Singer and His Song

I used to go to my grandmothers at the Bridge Hotel at Newton Cap and, I can remember, the men used to sing. One man called Lal Middlemiss used to sing a song called 'The Man in the Dirty Overcoat'. I don't remember what it was about but I would like to get a copy of it.

Sybil Gibson

A Close Community

My aunt lived at Fylands which, in the 1920s, was a community with its own football team. The women had a matting club at St Lukes church, where they used to make clippy mats. Its all gone now.

Vera Bradford

Saturday Matinee

Saturday afternoons were often spent at the hippodrome in Railway Street, the film usually being a Charlie Chaplin or a cowboy film. A bar of ever lasting toffee would see you through the whole performance. I remember there

Fylands Football Club.

Fylands Football team, in gala mood.

A bit of a masher. William Wood aged 21, in 1910.

Fylands Football team with their trophy for the 1921/22 season, along with members of the committee.

The Edgar Hall, Bishop Auckland. This was demolished to make way for the new bus station.

would sometimes be talent contests, which my brothers often entered. One of my brothers won a boxing contest and was offered either sweets or a jumper as a prize. He took the sweets, which didn't please my mother very much.

Marjorie Graham

A Bar Room Story

We used to sneak into the Hippodrome on a Saturday afternoon, because we didn't have any money. There used to be an ash toilet with a trap door, down the lane at the side, and one of us, the smallest, would climb through the trap door and up the hole in the toilet seat. He would then hide behind the curtain, which covered the door, and quietly open the door to let the others in. We would then find a seat and sit down to watch the film, that is unless the man who kept the kids under control saw us and then he would throw us out.

George Granby

Dances

There used to be dances in the Edgar Hall, for children, on Saturday afternoons run by Mr Alpin and Miss Owensworth. It cost sixpence and sometimes we had fancy dress dances. Miss Owensworth and Mr Alpin

Fancy dress for the children at the Edgar Hall, in the 1920s.

eventually got married so it was Mr and Mrs Alpin. When we got older there were the CLB dances (Church Lads Brigade). They were in the Edgar Hall and they were only sixpence. There was always a cloakroom to put your coat, you paid a penny and you had your ticket. They had sixpenny dances in St Peters. They had dances in the Drill Hall, but my mother wouldn't let us go.

Amy Hodgson

Cinemas

The Lyric Picture House, which became Herdman's shop and is now a video shop, was owned by Mrs Vart and the piano was played by Joan Neasham. When somebody died you went into full mourning for a year and then into half mourning for six months. You weren't allowed to go to places of entertainment. I remember after my grandfather died my cousin asked me to go to the Odeon picture. We had to ask my mother who was not very happy because we were still in mourning, but eventually she let me go.

Amy Hodgson

The Theatre

I found these programmes from the Bishop Auckland theatre almost seventy years ago, which I was going to discard as I am now in my eighty-eighth year. I enjoyed many happy and enjoyable evenings at the theatre. I

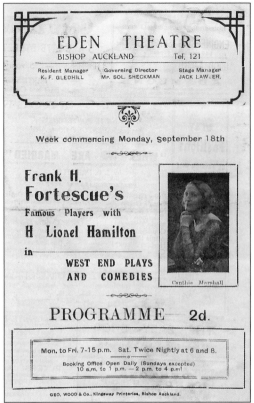

Above: A programme for the Repertory Company, which was very popular in the 1950s.

Above Right: This is a programme from one of the popular nude shows, which were held at the Eden Theatre in Bishop Auckland, in the 1950s.

fear the town has deteriorated since my youth.

M. Jarrett

Jane

My father-in-law was the stage manager at the Eden Theatre in the 1950s. There was a lot of nude shows at that time and one of them was Jane, the *Daily Mirror* cartoon character. My husband used to help his father backstage, but when Jane was on he was made to go and stand outside until she had finished her act. The girls in those days were not allowed to move when they were posing and the stage hands used to get up to all sorts of tricks to try to make them move. We had the shop opposite the theatre stage door and sold sweets and tobacco.

Mrs V. Rawle

Seen from The Gods

I worked for a short time, in the 1950s, on the limes [spotlights], up in the gallery at the Eden Theatre and my brother operated the lights. One of the acts I remember was Morris & Cowley, two comedians. They stuck in my mind and I can still remember one of the songs they sang:

> Good people here as you can see,
> We are members of the MCC
> Where Mr Hammond said with pride
> These are the lads of the English side

Bob Dockray

Table Tennis

We started the first table tennis club, in Bishop Auckland, in 1945. We played in the Toc H room behind the Queens Head Hotel. I was the treasurer, the first members were Cherry Fawcett, the councillor, Harold Dean, the manager of Maurices fur shop, a Pole called Braukukus - he was a very good player, Frank Penteland, the printer, Jock Hunter, an insurance man and Freddie Whitham, who worked in Elgies wood yard.

Bill Taylor Snr

Pig Keeping

George Roddam lived at Fylands, he kept pigs in the 1920s. The one he was most proud of was Jennie. She had lots of litters, but they were good friends and she followed him about. Keeping pigs was a hobby, as well as providing food for the family. They used to feed them with the kitchen remains all boiled up, but you can't do that now.

Vera Bradford

Morris & Cowley were two comedians who appeared at the Eden Theatre in the 1950s.

Knitting

The women of West Auckland used to use knitting sticks. They were made of wood and were often beautifully carved by their intended, as a love token. One of the sticks hooked into the skirt top and the other had a hole down the middle to take a needle so that they could knit with one hand. I have a pair of knitting sticks that belonged to my aunt.

Vera Bradford

George Roddam poses proudly with his prize pig, Jennie.

Knitting sticks, used by the ladies of West Auckland.

Dyed eggs are produced in the district at Easter time. Competitions are held for both dyed and painted eggs.

Dyed Eggs

At Easter we dyed eggs by boiling them with coloured cloth or onion skins. Some people used to wrap them in pieces of lace curtains, so that the pattern of the lace was transferred onto the egg. Sometimes you used leaves and flowers fastened to the egg before you boiled it to make patterns. There were competitions for the best dyed egg.

Vera Bradford

Leading Man

I remember the first show I ever saw, it was a pantomime in a wooden hut. I went with my sister but we hadn't enough money to get in, but a man who was a commercial traveller paid for us to go in. When my mother found out she was very angry and insisted on giving him the money. He became a very good friend of the family for many years after that. My father was very clever and taught himself French, Spanish and the trombone. My first introduction to theatre was I suppose at the Eden Theatre, seeing plays and shows. I wanted to speak properly and went for lessons for many years to Mrs Margaret Marshal at Durham.

I did a lot of shows, with Mrs Chandos Craddock as producer. I was once on a plane going to Ireland and she was sitting nearby. She was talking to someone sitting near her and she said 'That young man over there is one of the best leads I've ever worked with.'

Above: This picture of Mrs Craddock, in 1924, was taken from the programme of the Bishop Auckland YMCA Amateur Operatic Society's production of *The Mikado*.

Above Right: Mr Chandos Craddock was the musical director of the 1924 production of *The Mikado*.

That was me. I took all the leading parts in the operatic shows.

William 'Billy' Drysdale

[*Mrs Craddock produced musicals in Bishop Auckland for many years, with her husband as musical director. Her last production was Ruddigore, in 1964, when she was over ninety years old.*]

Bishop Auckland Youth Choir

We held rehearsals in the Girls Grammar School. John Taylor was the conductor and Margaret Taylor,

his wife, was the accompanist. The solo soprano was Mary Hogg, Doreen Andrews the solo contralto and Ronnie Owers the solo tenor. We gave concerts in Bishop Auckland town hall and every year we gave a concert at Redcar, which was always a sell out.

Jean Boyle

Broadcasts

The first broadcast of the Bishop Auckland Youth Choir was on New Years Day, 1947 recorded in the Baths Hall, Darlington and Dame Flora

William Drysdale, as the Duke of Plazatoro, in
a production of *The Gondoliers* by the Bishop
Auckland Operatic Society.

The Bishop Auckland Youth Choir with conductor John Taylor. His wife Margaret was the
accompanist.

Wilfred Pickles and his wife Mabel were stars of the popular radio show 'Have a Go' which was once broadcast from Bishop Auckland. Wilfreds catch phrases were 'What's on the table Mabel?' and 'Give 'im the money Barney'.

Robson took part in that broadcast. It was so good that it was broadcast locally and it was broadcast nationally after that. They did 'Have A Go', with Wilfred Pickles, in the Kings Hall Café in Bishop and the choir performed during the show. They also did 'Workers Playtime', with Ronnie Hilton, at West Auckland Clothing Factory. They did broadcasts in 'What Cheer Geordie', with Willy Walker and his band.

There was eight of the ladies from the choir called the Melody Maids who were used in broadcasts such as 'The Airs The Limit'. Some of the recording was done in the Co-op hall in Darlington, but the majority were done at the town hall, Gosforth. On the 4 September 1955, they did a broadcast from Bishop Auckland town hall on the BBC Home Service. In all, the choir did thirty-one broadcasts. The choir gave a charity performance at Richmond, in Yorkshire, with Vic Oliver and Heddle Nash. Vic Oliver usually left after he had performed, but he was so impressed with the Youth Choir that he stood at the back of the theatre to hear them sing. In 1948 they sang at a charity concert in aid of the Easington Colliery disaster fund, organised by the Mayor of Darlington. Ada Allsop heard about it and gave her services free. They became the Vinovium Singers in about 1952 when all the people got married.

Kath Sewell

Choral Society

The Vinovium Singers came to a crossroads in 1956. They were preparing this thing called 'The Music Makers', by Edward Elgar and it went off very well indeed and it was decided to form the Bishop Auckland & District Choral Society. Kath and I joined in 1955, when they recruited more mature singers.

Jim Sewell

[*The very first performance of 'The Music Makers' was in St Peters church, Bishop Auckland and was conducted by Sir Edward Elgar himself. He was a personal friend of local musician, Dr Nicholas Kilburn. Subsequently the piece was repeated with the Leeds Symphony Orchestra and the Felling Male Voice Choir, in Bishop Auckland town hall.*]

The Beer Crate Elijah

In 1956, the first oratorio we gave was a performance of 'Elijah', in Wesley church, Bishop Auckland. The choir by this time, with helpers, was about one hundred strong and we needed put in rostra, for those at the back to stand on. It was arranged with Jones', the lemonade people, to lend us some lemonade crates. On the Tuesday night we had to strip down the stage, as there was a funeral the next day. The crates, far from being lemonade crates, were Worthington, Bass, Tetleys Yorkshire Bitter and Tadcaster Ales and were put in the corridor at the back. We sustained a rocket from one of the senior members of the church, 'what's

BISHOP AUCKLAND AND DISTRICT
CHORAL SOCIETY
AND
BISHOP AUCKLAND ORCHESTRA

AUTUMN CONCERT

in

The Technical College, Bishop Auckland,

on

Tuesday, 26th November, 1963.

Soloists:

NORMA PROCTER
(CONTRALTO)

TOM HALL
(TENOR)

Conductor.................John W. R. Taylor.
Accompanist.................Margaret E. Taylor.
Leader.................Daphne Nicholson

A joint concert, of the Bishop Auckland Choral Society with the Bishop Auckland Orchestra. The choral society was founded in 1956. The orchestra enjoyed varying fortunes over the years. For some time the orchestra consisted of string instruments, but it was reformed as a full orchestra when Mr John Taylor took over as the conductor, in 1961. Miss Daphne Nicholson was the leader from 1956.

the meaning of this, don't you realise there is a temperance meeting coming out?' For ever after in the Choral Society, that was known as the beer crate Elijah.

Jim Sewell

eaten at a tea party held in the Bay Horse Hotel, in Fore Bondgate.

Peggy Wicks

Lurchers

There were different crosses of lurcher, depending on what was wanted. It all depended on what kind of game they were after. Whippets are very fast and ideal for rabbits, but if you were wanting to race hares that would be no good because it would be too small and hadn't enough stamina. But cross it with a Saluki, which was used for chasing gazelles in the desert, they were very good hare dogs because they had no common sense. They had no brains and all they could do was run, they'll run themselves to death if you let them, where a whippet has the common sense to stop when it is tired. Greyhounds are very fast, but have no staying power, so you cross a greyhound with a Saluki which has the staying power. In the olden days they had what was called a 'snack', which was a mixture. They were just used for killing food. It was a way of living. If a dog didn't kill for food it was no good and not worth its keep.

Years ago me dad had lurchers which would kill five or six hares a day. The travellers would set a camp up and let the dog go over the fence and bring back food for that night. In the old days it was an old fella going out with his dog, kill a hare and bring it home for the pot. At one time me dad would go miles to buy a good lurcher for maybe three and a half pound. Nowadays you are talking an absolute fortune, because it has become a sport rather

The Bay Horse Hotel, in Fore Bondgate, where the girls held their tea party after collecting money from the mid-Summer cushions.

Midsummer Cushions

I wanted to raise money for the charity, ME and thought it would be nice to resurrect the old, eighteenth century Bishop Auckland custom of midsummer cushions. It was traditional for the girls of the town to prepare stools, covered in clay, on which they designed patterns with flower heads, seeds and leaves. Then they sat at the corner of each street on midsummer day, with a pewter collecting plate for the contributions of passers by. There was great competition among the girls to produce the most attractive cushion. Later in the day the girls bought tansy cakes, which were than a means of getting your dinner, which it was when you were on the road travelling. In the old days, if you had a bad week and you couldn't make no money, two pounds a week was an absolute fortune. If you couldn't make money, you could go out and take game and that was the family life with that lurcher. Most of them would walk alongside the caravan, they didn't need a kennel, they didn't need tying up, they were just there to the word and would go off and get food.

Eddie Shields

Sunday School

The first contact I had with any church was when I was taken to Sunday school at the Wesley church in Bishop Auckland. I sat in a lovely child-size chair of a kind that I had never seen before and the teacher, Miss Atherton, was very nice to me. I may have been around four or five at the time. We sang hymns and said prayers - 'Jesus bids us shine' and 'When He cometh to take up his jewels'. Some time later I was in the proper Sunday school with a lugubrious, self-important superintendent called Ferens. His name appeared on flour bags at home because he still ran the mill on the Gaunless, near the market place. Although, I imagine the water wheel that powered the grindstones had been replaced by then. I had what seemed an incredibly ancient man teaching our small group, Mr Harrison, with a fringe of white hair around his otherwise bald pate, and a quiet patient manner. Later still, I had the man who was to teach me German at the grammar school,

Arthur Wise. Even later, he married my first delightful Miss Artherton (Betty) and they had a family.

Apart from the very small children who had a little room to themselves, Sunday school was held in the main part of the church, not an ideal location because it was a bit like an open-plan office. Sunday school seemed to consist of parables, stories with a moral, and learning pieces out of the Bible for the anniversary. It never occurred to me whose anniversary it was, it just came round at regular intervals - like Easter, Harvest Festival, Rememberance Sunday and Christmas. I guess it must have been the church's anniversary. Anyway, we learned pieces of scripture or even whole psalms. I once did the one that starts, 'I will lift up mine eyes unto the hills' (although it says 'mountains' in the copy I now have). As we became more expert, we were trusted with parts in the annual Nativity play - a charming mixture of prose, verse and music, with lots of home-made costumes and stage lighting.

Ken Walton

We Dob, Dob, Dob

I don't know how old I was when I joined the Cubs, but we met in one of the Wesley school rooms, possibly the one where I first sat in my little chair and wanted to be a sunbeam. Our pack leader was a sensible and well organised woman, Vera Carr, who ran a wool shop in the town when she was not baring her teeth as Akela. I learned to tie bowlines and sheep-shanks and how to stop my laces coming undone.

I could semaphore at the rate of about four letters a minute, enough to send a message in the course of an hour or so, but Morse defeated me. I discovered, on an evening trip along the River Wear, how to make something vaguely resembling pancakes but without eggs, just flour and water. I never saw these culinary delights before or since. My skill at fire lighting was my pride and joy for years. Eventually I got too old for the Cubs. I had over stayed my time there and it was the season to move on into the Scouts - the 7th Bishop Auckland troop. I had barely found my way around them when I was called by a siren voice from another establishment - the Central Methodist church. This appeared to have several advantages. Firstly it was nearer home than Wesley, only about half the distance, but the chief attraction was that as well as Sunday school, there was a youth club - with girls! We switched alliance overnight. We must have been twelve or thirteen.

Ken Walton

The Club

The Central Primitive Methodist church (the Prims) ran a number of activities. The youth club had only been running a few years, meeting on Thursday evenings between 7 and 10. An under-14 club had been formed to cope with those who were thought to be too young for the main club. This is where I started. There was a fairly active Boys Brigade Company. I joined this too. It [the club] ran in the central schoolroom, the main room in the building, apart

from the church itself, and in some of the rooms off the main corridor. One of these was a billiard room, housing a quarter-size table in what had been, during the war, an air-raid wardens post. A typical evening at the club would start off with a few folk, mostly lads of course, drifting in and setting up the table tennis tables. Others would play billiards or snooker. There was a crude, but robust, record turntable, amplifier and free-standing speaker in a small room opening off the schoolroom. Those who wanted played records. The more affluent brought in their weeks new record purchases to show off to the admiring company. Those with a leaning towards electrics tinkered with the amplifier to improve its performance. Around eight o'clock, the boys would repair to the billiard room for a discussion group. The girls stayed in the main schoolroom for needlework and other such feminine pursuits, which says a lot about their social role at the time. At nine o'clock the discussion group broke up, which was a signal for the girls to pack up too. The tables were cleared and some games and dancing completed the evening.

Socials were some of the high points of the calendar. The schoolroom was cleared of tables and its benches moved, some around the walls and some in adjacent rooms. French chalk, or pounce, was sprinkled onto the wooden floor to improve the surface for dancing. Its effect was defeated to some extent by the nail heads that stuck up from the worn grain of the old boards. Refreshments were prepared in one of the side rooms, records piled in readiness beside the turntable, and folks started to arrive in their best clothes. Socials took two forms - church socials and club socials. For

Newfield String Band in the 1920s.

us the former were quite entertaining, but the club socials were really our scene. They consisted of a mixture of dancing and games. Games included musical chairs, statues, postman's knock, trencher and Hyde Park corner. I don't know whether any of these are still played in this sophisticated age. Some of them are harmless parlour games that were popular in Victorian times. Others, with hindsight, seem to have been designed to encourage intimate contact between the sexes. Perhaps our elders felt that if there was going to be intimate contact it might as well be under their control. They were wasting their time of course, but it was worth a try. Our chemistry teacher always referred to our youth club as the marriage bureau and a surprisingly large number of us married from the club, including me.

Ken Walton

Boys Brigade

More martial than the Scouts, these brigades always used to have a bugle corps that blasted down the main streets on ceremonial occasions, notably on Remembrance Sunday. Our brigade leaders were Edwin Rochester, who ran a painting business and whose wife played the violin at concerts, Maurice Hepples, who also held some rank in the Home Guard during the war and Alan Vickers, who had been a prefect in one of the upper forms at my school when I started. I set off one evening, in the summer of 1945, with the last two of these three, together with Johnny Atkinson and Ernie King, as an advance party to set up camp at Witton Mill, near Witton le Wear. We had an assortment of tents, of various ages and states of repair. The farmer who owned the land provided us with straw for our sacking palliasses. The first night was not too bad since the weather was fine and we had ample space to spread out in. The following day the rest of the troop arrived and we found ourselves sleeping like sardines, feet to the tent pole, head to the outside, and it rained. This wouldn't have been too bad except that our tent leaked and it kept on raining. In fact it rained for a lot of the week. By the end of the week, as a result of inhaling wood smoke day after day and sleeping in damp bedding, I could scarcely raise my voice over a croak. On the Friday afternoon my worried-looking father arrived, sent by my even more concerned mother. He took one look at me and insisted I collect my gear and go home with him there and then. I wasn't too sorry - this hadn't been an ideal introduction to camping. Incidentally, Japan had surrendered on the Wednesday and the war was finally over.

Ken Walton

CHAPTER 8

People remembered

Bill Oliver, and colleagues, with a captured Japanese tank. The men served together in Burma during the Second World War.

Bill in his greenhouse with his much beloved plants.

A Much Loved Photographer

Bill Oliver was one of the old style press photographers, who went to any lengths to get his pictures. He went out in all weathers, at first on a motor bike and sidecar, wearing motor cycle leathers and later in a *Northern Echo* van, carrying an old plate camera. The pictures were developed in a darkroom, at the back of the *Northern Echo* offices in Newgate Street, Bishop Auckland. Bill was famous for his battered tweed hat and his sometimes gentle, sometimes belligerent approach to those whose picture he was taking. He was particularly brusque with reporters who were not ready when he wanted to leave on a job. He drove the *Northern Echo* van in a manner that made young reporters fear for their lives. His persistence and dogged determination were particularly evident in his war service in the 3rd Dragoon Guards, with which he served throughout the Burma Campaign. He broke his glasses as the British Army were driven back to Imphal and finally got them repaired when the British forces retook Burma. Bill did not allow a shattered pair of glasses to stop his war.

A well known character in south west Durham, he became so well known that when Bishop Auckland Football Club played Crook Town, at the Kingsway ground, as the Bishop Auckland team took the field half the crowd cheered; when the Crook team appeared the other half cheered, but when Bill Oliver appeared, in his battered hat and riding mac, the whole crowd cheered him to his place behind the goal. I expect he would raise his hat to them as he always did. Not many people knew that Bill was an internationally famous photographer, winning prizes in competitions all over the world. His work was likened to Karsh of Ottowa, the internationally renowned portrait photographer. Beneath that battered hat was a man whose brusque Yorkshire manner hid a kindly man, who loved photography and took great pains to get a good picture.

The one thing about Bill was that he treated everybody the same, no matter who they were. On one occasion he was late to take the picture of the Queen Mother at Bowes Museum. He went over to her and said, 'Come over here luv and I'll take your picture.' He got his picture. On another occasion we were on holiday in London and we went to a service in St Pauls Cathedral and sat in the back row. The service was for the life boat anniversary and royalty were there. At the rear of the royal procession was Mrs Michael Ramsey, with the wife of the Bishop of London. She stopped, looked at Bill sitting there and said, 'Hello Mr Oliver. What are you doing here? Michael is just disrobing, you must wait and see him.' Michael Ramsey was the Archbishop of Canterbury and had been the Bishop of Durham. Bill used to go to Auckland Castle and play chess with him. Bill loved his garden and spent many happy hours, taking as much care over his plants as he did over his photography.

Audrey Oliver

Allswop

This was the nickname of a porter, who worked on Bishop Auckland railway station. He used to shout 'all swop', instead of the more usual 'all change'. He walked around the town for many years. He had long flowing white hair and never did anyone any harm.

Margorie Graham

Spanish Onion Sellers

Every year the Spanish onion sellers used to come round Bishop Auckland. They used to go round the streets with strings of onions hanging from their bicycles.

Amy Hodgson

Gold and Diamonds

I was only three on the only occasion I saw my grandfather, Jeremiah Addison, before he died on 24 March 1934. But the aura that surrounded my being ushered in to see him, lying on a chaise lounge, left a lasting impression that he was someone very special. Indeed he was, for he had a fascinating life. Jeremiah was a typical Victorian, being a strict disciplinarian - woe betide any child who was late for a meal - with a pioneering spirit. He was too, a very skilled cabinet maker and a great lover of the countryside. Jeremiah, his brother Robert and his sister Frances inherited from their father the Black Boy Inn, at Canney Hill, which was sold for the brothers to buy

When Baptised.	Child's Christian Name	Parent's Name.		Abode.	Quality, Trade, or Profession.	By whom the Ceremony was performed
		Christian.	Surname.			
1902 13 Feb No. 641	Alice Maud	Thomas Henry & Jane Ann	Rudd	6 High Bondgate	Railway Porter	W J Wingate Vicar
1902 20 Feb No. 642	Annie Eliza	Henry Frank & Annie	Lind	34 Edward St Peters		W J Wingate Vicar
1902 21 Feb No. 643	Charles Edward	Charles William & Mary Jane	Hay	27 South Terr	Coke Drawer	W J Wingate Vicar

This records the baptism of a child of Dr Frank Lind and Eliza Bragger.

the Theatre Royal, Bishop Auckland - later the Eden Theatre. Robert ran it, but Jeremiah emigrated to South Africa, where he was followed by his wife Sarah. He designed and built the first diamond washing machine for the De Beers mine at Kimberley. Then he built a gold washing machine, driven by a huge wheel on the River Vaal. Within days of starting operations the lot was swept away by floods. A working replica of this machine was used in the play *A Woman's Victory*, seen at the Bishop Auckland theatre in 1895, when Jeremiah advised on its design. Sarah opened a general store in Kimberley, supplying the miners. It prospered so much that later both had to run it. Sarah also laid the foundation to the wealth the couple amassed, by acting as banker to the native chiefs. They

trusted her more than the banks.

Jeremiah returned to England from time to time and, on one of his voyages back to South Africa, was shipwrecked at St Helena. He and Sarah came back to England for the last time in 1887, believed to be due to the dry dust in South Africa affecting his chest. On the other hand they had made enough money for him never to work again - with the exception of owning, for a short time, the Cumberland Arms at Brickyard [a village near Close House]. They next lived over Doggarts department store in Newgate Street, Bishop Auckland before moving to 15 Clarence Street. Jeremiah also rented Shull Cottage at Bedburn, near Hamsterley for holidays, when he hired a bus to take the whole family and their provisions. Here he enjoyed the countryside and would offer half a crown - a lot of money then - if they could identify any birds. What a pity he never wrote his life story. I am, however, making amends. This is but a snippet of the chapter on him in my book. I am writing the family history, a lot of which involves the Bishop Auckland area.

Vernon Addison

Disappearing Magicians

Eliza Bragger was the daughter of a theatrical boarding house keeper in Vickers Street, Bishop Auckland. She was particularly attracted to stage magicians and 'married' three of them and had children to them all. Like all good stage magicians they disappeared, leaving Eliza with the children. One of the offspring of Dr Lind was christened at St Peters church on 20 February 1902. The baptismal entry shows him as actor. Eliza had acted as his assistant in his act. Eliza's sister (my great-grandmother) married John Inman in 1871. Dr Lind ran off to Glasgow, with a lady from the chorus of *The Belle of New York*, who he abandoned in Glasgow with another set of children. Eliza subsequently went on the stage herself, as a clairvoyant, but one cannot help wondering if she had had such foresight why she didn't foresee the disappearance of her partners. In the 1940s the Glasgow family contacted the Bishop Auckland family and they met, but the meeting was not a success as they had nothing in common but a philandering father.

Margaret Taylor

Dr Frank Lind, magician.

A Charlatan

Dr H. Frank Lind wrote a book on stage magic, as Professor Henri Garenne, called, *The Art of Modern Conjuring*, in 1886, which he had plagiarized from Professor Hoffman's, *Modern Magic*, written in 1876. He appeared at the Princes Hall in Piccadilly, London, in March 1888 - announcing that he had been before the public for twenty-four years. He was in the provinces the previous year and continued giving conjuring and anti-spiritualistic entertainment until 1895.

Edwin A. Dawes

Arthur Jefferson, with his family, c. 1896. They had recently left Bishop Auckland.

[*Dr Lind appeared at the Eden Theatre and the town hall, Bishop Auckland on many occasions with his magic act. He no doubt boarded with Eliza's mother, in Vickers Street.*]

Quoth the Raven

In the 1920s Arthur Jefferson, the father of Stan Laurel, managed the Eden Theatre in Bishop Auckland. He used to stand outside when the first house was leaving. He wore a dress suit and a top hat, the hat was blocked by Mr Mason, the hatter next door to the theatre, for two free tickets.

Mr Jefferson used to say goodnight to the people leaving and say, 'have you seen my lad at the Kings Hall?' He was very proud of Stan. Arthur Jefferson had a very bad temper. His office was on the corner, up a short flight of stairs. On Saturday nights the touring manager of the company that had been performing that week would come up to the office after the show to collect the money. Sometimes Arthur would complain about the standard of the show and a row would break out. He would lose his temper and throw the manager down the stairs. He would then write comments in the account book for that week and if the show was bad he wrote 'Quoth the Raven' [from the poem by Edgar Alan Poe 'Quoth the Raven, never more'] and he would not employ that company again. He would sometimes sack people and on the Monday ask for them and couldn't understand why they weren't there.

Percy Ewbank

[*Arthur Jefferson managed the Eden Theatre twice, from 1889 to 1896 and from 1921 to 1925. Percy Ewbank was the accountant for the theatre and subsequently the general manager.*]

A Real Tradgedy

When the Eden Theatre was built, my grandfather was killed falling off the roof. Someone had to go and tell my grandmother. The foreman went to the house and knocked on the door, 'Are you the widow X?' My grandmother said she was Mrs X and the man said, 'Well you're the widow

The Eden Theatre, Bishop Auckland has since been demolished. Here we see the corner above which Arthur Jefferson had his office. This corner was, and still is, a regular meeting place for the people of Bishop Auckland. Theatres have occupied this site since 1863.

X now, your husband has just fallen off the theatre roof.' My grandmother just asked him to knock next door and ask the neighbour to come in.

Anonymous

[*This story was told to the contractors when the Eden Theatre was being pulled down, in 1974. A lady stood watching the demolition and told this very sad tale. She left without giving her name.*]

Trapeze Artiste

My cousin Peggy married a man called Tobias Van Den Berg, he was a trapeze artiste. His partner was called

up in the First World War so he trained Peggy in the act. I remember being taken to the Hippodrome, in Railway Street to see them perform in 1923.

Vera Bradford

The Drummonds

Mr and Mrs Drummond lived in a big, white house, behind St Helens. I worked for them until the war. They had cinemas at Seahouses, Middleton in Teesdale and the Hippodrome, the Kings Hall and the Eden Theatre in Bishop Auckland. Mrs Drummond came from Lucker in Northumberland and Mr Drummond

119

Above: Peggy Van den Berg with her pet dog.
Above Right: Peggy with her children, in the 1920s.

was a Scot, or his mother was. My Uncle Bert was the cook/butler, he also acted as chauffeur and drove their big maroon Chevrolet. The gardeners name was Aitiss. Mrs Drummond was a real lady, she had four dogs, Nero, Judy and two little dogs - one was called Peter and she always carried one of the little ones under her arm wherever she went. Every year they went to Lucker, because her father lived there, or to Middleton for two or three weeks and I went with them. They also had goats, which had to be milked. Mrs Drummond was the brains of the business. She died first and he remarried.

Alice Dowson

A Very Famous Girl

My father remembers Julie Andrews coming into the café, when she was a little girl, for ice cream. Her mother and step-father, Barbara and Ted Andrews, were appearing at the Eden Theatre, opposite.

Eddie Rossi

Born in a Trunk

I went to Cockton Hill school and was the call boy at the Eden Theatre and used to look after Julie Andrews while her father and mother were on

120

EDEN THEATRE, Bishop Auckland

Week commencing MONDAY, MARCH 5th, 1945
MONDAY to FRIDAY, Continuous from 6 to 9-45 p.m.
SATURDAY, Three Performances, 2, 6 and 8 p.m.

A. J. L. PRODUCTIONS present

RADIO INTERNATIONAL

A Galaxy of International Stars!

TED ANDREWS
and BARBARA

The Canadian Troubadours and Famous BBC Stars

MICHELLE	CRONY SCOTT
SISTERS Your Girl Friends	A Fool's Mate

JOE VINCENT & FLO "Have a Go, Joe"

ALAN KAYE	CARMEN
and PARTNER The Mexican Juggler	Spanish Accordionist

KHARKOV	STAN JAY and JOAN
THE RUSSIAN ILLUSIONIST	Too Funny with Words

Geo. H. Field & Son, Thornton Road, Bradford. Tel. 858.

Above: Programme advertising the appearance of Ted and Barbara Andrews, the mother and stepfather of Julie Andrews.

Above Right: Roy Pattinson rose from working as a callboy at the Eden Theatre, via Bishop Auckland Operatic Society, to become a professional actor and singer. He has appeared in many West End musicals such as *Finnians Rainbow, Oliver* and *Guys and Dolls*. His television roles were in the *Onedin Line, The Likely Lads*, and *When The Boat Comes In*. Roy has appeared in a number of films including The *Dirty Dozen, A Bridge Too Far* and *Charge of the Light Brigade*. His work as a performer has taken him as far afield as Turkey, South Africa and Kenya.

stage. Julie was about four years old at the time. I eventually went on the stage myself, as a singer, and was in the cast of *Guys and Dolls* that appeared in the Coronation Royal Command Performance. Since then I have been in various television series such as *The Likely Lads* and *When The Boat Comes In*.

Roy Pattinson

Bullet Holes

There were what was thought to be bullet holes in the wall of the foyer of the Eden Theatre, when I was a call boy there. Somebody fired a revolver in the foyer and the holes were there for a long time afterwards.

Roy Pattinson

[*This may link with a story that the foyer*

121

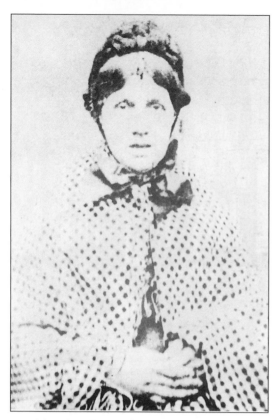

Mary Ann Cotton, the infamous West Auckland poisoner.

of the Eden Theatre was believed to be haunted and that a ghost could sometimes be seen passing through.]

Sixty Glorious Years

Of all the people I worked with, in my years as an amateur drama and operatic producer, the one who will always stand out in my memory is Clary Young. Clary had started his singing career as a boy in St Peters church choir and continued to be a member until shortly before he died. He was also a very loyal member of the male chorus of some of the operatic societies in the area. I first came across Clary when I did my first musical production in Newton Aycliffe, in 1964. I was taken to meet Mrs Chandos Craddock, rehearsing Bishop Auckland Operatic Society's production of *Ruddigore* in the grammar school, which was performed in the Temperane Hall. I then saw Shildon Operatic Society's production of *Desert Song* at the Shildon Hippodrome and to my surprise I recognised a gentleman of the chorus who was in both shows - Clary Young. He stood out because, despite the change of costume, he always took the same position on stage - down stage right. He was always the smallest of the tenors and had for some fifty years of productions been in that position. One night, during rehearsals of *The Mikado* at Newton Aycliffe, Clary turned up. I had foolishly commented to a friend that if it was left to me I would get him to move elsewhere on stage. This became a challenge, but with a slip in concentration one night he managed to get into his usual position, 1-0 to Clary. For my next production, *Gondoliers*, I worked the moves out carefully and won, a one all draw. *The Merry Widow* and Clary shot into the down stage right position, 2-1 to Clary. He was a loyal and reliable gentleman of the chorus for sixty years, earning a fifty year and bar medal from the National Operatic & Dramatic Association, although as far as I know, he never took a leading part.

I have a very warm spot for 'down stage right' as I called him. I am sure that if I go to heaven, in the chorus of angels will be Clary Young - down stage right, of course.

John Land

The West Auckland Poisoner

My grandmother's sister brought up Mary Ann Cotton's daughter, in Ferryhill. My grandmother kept a pub next door to where Mary Ann lived in West Auckland and we had a jug that Mary Ann gave to my grandmother.

Sonny Dowthwaite

[*Mary Ann Cotton was the infamous West Auckland poisoner, whose execution was delayed because she was having a baby. After the birth Mary Ann was executed in Durham goal on 24 March 1873, for the poisoning of her bigamous husband, Charles Edward Cotton. The case aroused great curiosity because it was thought she had murdered at least eighteen people, for the insurance money, and had four husbands who had died in suspicious circumstances, as well as having a number of lovers.*]

Street Entertainers

A blind violinist used to stand and play at Gregorie's corner. Ned Gibson, the son of the Durham miners poet, played the harp at the corner of Gibb Chare and a man called Wright used to sometimes sing with him. He also went round the villages playing for money. He made the harp himself and gave it to my brother. We had it for years but it went in the sale room along with a lot of other things. There were two men used to play a barrel organ in Newgate Street, they were called Dundas - Eddie and Freddie.

Amy Hodgson

Born in the Town Hall

My father, Hughie Wharton, was born in Bishop Auckland and my mother Lottie Wharton was born in Coundon, as I was myself. My husband, John Clarke, was also born in Bishop Auckland. My mother and father lived in a flat in the town hall and were the caretakers. Also living there was my sister, Beatrice ,and my brother, Hughie. My husband was in the RAF, at Leeming, and we lived in private accommodation in Bedale. In October 1954 my husband was posted to Germany. As married quarters were very hard to get and I was expecting my first baby, I moved back to live with my parents in the town hall. As babies in those days were born at home, I decided on a home birth. Bernadette was born on 22 January 1955, in the flat in the town hall. Councillor Bob Middlewood told us that she was the first child ever to be born there. Bernadette is married now and has two children of her own - Tanya and David.

Kathleen Clarke

United Buses

The first United buses used to go to Cabin Gate. The conductor was Edgar Hobson and he used to shout 'penny all the way!' It cost a penny from the market place to Cabin Gate in those days. Featherstone and Griffiths buses went to Etherley and Stevensons buses to Toft Hill.

Amy Hodgson

The Prince of Wales is pictured on a visit to the North East.

A road gang takes a breather in Newgate Street.

The Batts Mission

There was a mission down on the Batts, at Bishop Auckland. The pastor, a grey-haired man, used to stand on Saturday afternoons at Briathwaites corner, playing hymns on his accordion. People gave him coppers. My piano, that was bought at Tiplady's sale room in Cockton Hill Road, for £45, was given to the Batts Mission and Gill's furniture shop delivered it free of charge. My husband and me were invited to the dedication of the piano, by the Bishop of Jarrow, at the Batts Mission. Somebody else gave an organ. The piano was a walnut Berlin & Mansfield and had brass candle holders. The Batts Mission is now converted into a bungalow.

Vera Bradford

The Man Who Wouldn't Be King

The Prince of Wales passed through Coundon, during the depression in the 1930s. My mother went down to Bishop to see if she could see him. I stayed at home to do the housework. I was black leading the fireplace and I ran out of paraffin, so I put my coat on and went to the shop near the War Memorial in Coundon. As I came out there was a procession of cars and I stood there and saw the prince go by. My mother never saw him.

Flo Hall

Repairs were being carried out on the railway lines, here in the old goods yard, behind the Methodist church in Newgate Street, Bishop Auckland c. 1930.

Prince Of The People

The Prince of Wales visited Nutters Buildings [near Middlestone Moor]. The buildings were made of wood. He stopped and spoke to the people there. I remember a picture in the paper of them leaning over the gates talking to the prince.

Vera Bradford

A Loyal Crowd

When we lived at Etherley, the King and Queen came past our

Miss Nellie Welford is seen here after being healed by Pastor Jeffrey, in Bishop Auckland Town Hall. She had previously been carried to the meetings on the stretcher.

gate and there was George's mother and I and George's brother. We all had our flags and we got a wave all on our own. They had come to Witton Park station. It was after 1936 when we moved to Etherley, so it would have been George VI and Queen Elizabeth, the present Queen Mother.

Amy Hodgson

An Early Morning Call

I was a reporter for the *Northern Echo* and one morning, about eight o'clock, I got a call, at home, from Clary Simons, a contact who lived at Witton Park, telling me that the royal train was at Witton Park station, with the Queen Mother on board. He had been round the village and told everybody and the children and a crowd had gone round to the station to look. She was up here to open the 150th anniversary celebration of the opening of the Stockton & Darlington railway, at Shildon. Witton Park station was often used as a siding when royalty visited the area. I can't help wondering what the Queen Mother thought when she looked out to find the villagers all standing there.

Marie Land

The Evangelist

I talked to many older members of the Assembly of God Pentecostal church and learned of the 'miracles of Bishop Auckland town hall', in 1927. Local Pentecostals invited evangelist, Stephen Jeffrey, to preach in the town for six weeks. Initially, only a handful of local Pentecostals attended. However, it wasn't long before people were coming from miles around to see and hear what was taking place. It was recorded that, 'as many as 1,500 were turned away after waiting in the queue for hours. In the hall was a sight never to be forgotten, packed to suffocation, platform, staircases, rooms and hundreds were turned away disappointed.'

During the services there was outstanding healing of people born blind, helpless cripples and many inflicted with all manner of diseases. 'Cripples the doctors couldn't cure' was

This is a queue around the Town Hall, Bishop Auckland, in 1927. The eagerly awaited event was a meeting held by the Evangelist, Pastor Jeffrey.

the headline in the *Northern Echo* of the time. Mrs Stead from West Auckland was a road accident victim, who could not walk. She was able to walk unaided for the first time after attending pastor Jeffrey's service. Nellie Welford, from Evenwood, was unable to walk or speak and was taken to the town hall on a stretcher. Pastor Jeffrey came down the stairs and prayed for her. Within an hour of returning home the symptoms began to disappear. Nellie went on the attend meetings all over the country to tell people of her miracle cure.

Catherine Simpson (née Pentland)

The Whittons of Witton Park

Edith Hall was the eldest of four children, born to Dennis and Cicely Whitton in 1921. She had two sisters, Margaret (Peggy) and Jean (who died in childhood, in 1935) and a brother Kenneth. All were educated in the recently demolished school. At the outbreak of World War Two, Edith joined the Land Army, working locally to help the war effort and eventually joining the Womens Royal Air Force. When she was twenty-six, in 1947, Edith married Charles Hall, who had a haulage contract business. She later went on to have her own business in the shape of a mobile café. This was a converted bus and she could be relied on to be there to provide refreshments to travellers passing Witton le Wear, parked in a lay-by on the main road [A 68] and inevitably wearing a woolly hat. Her father, Dennis, will probably be remembered as having a sweet shop and, later, a billiard room further down the street in Park Road, Witton Park.

Cicely Whitton, Edith's mother, was very well known to Witton Park residents, having played a central role in local politics and standing as a Progressive candidate for the Escomb ward, alongside William Chater and Fred Dowson. She was the first woman

VOTE FOR

CICELY WHITTON

WILLIAM CHAYTOR

FRED DOWSON

Above: Edith Whitton, seen in her WAAF uniform, with her sister Peggy. The little boy is their cousin, Brian Milburn, who grew up to run Clarendon Motors in the town. Also pictured is Bunty, the dog.
Above Right: This is an election pamphlet for Cicely Whitton, who stood as a candidate for the Urban District Council elections, which were held on 10 May 1949.

councillor on the Bishop Auckland Urban Council. Edith died in 1988 and, among her belongings, she left behind a documented history she had researched and written on Witton Park.

Del Smith